Beyond The Collar

Mark Edwards

© Mark Edwards 2021

Faithbuilders Publishing
12 Dukes Court, Bognor Road,
Chichester, PO19 8FX, United Kingdom
www.faithbuilderspublishing.com

ISBN: 978-1-913181-73-4

British Library Cataloguing in Publication Data. A catalogue record for this book is available from the British Library

Formatted by Faithbuilders Publishing
Cover by Esther Kotecha, EKDesign
Printed in the United Kingdom

CONTENTS

DEDICATION

I dedicate this book to my wife Lesley

Thank you for your unwavering love and steadfast resilience

without which I might have given up.

You are the closest I can get to God in the flesh, my Angel.

I love you more than words can describe.

ENDORSEMENTS

Mark's story does for parish life what James Herriot did for vets, a pacey, fluent, irresistible read with a Tiggerish bounce, nakedly candid, forthright and impressive.

Quentin Letts
Theatre Critic
Newspaper Columnist

Mark Edwards takes the reader on a personal emotional roller-coaster, while conveying what it's like to be a vicar in a Northern industrial town.

The Independent

A real pager turner.

The Guardian

A powerful, honest autobiography.

The Telegraph

Courageous and inspiring.

The Times

This is a very honest book and a good read.

Lorraine Kelly (ITV)

An exceptionally good read.

Mark Woods (former editor of the Baptist Times)

Mark Edwards' life story has covered so many extremes that there are moments where you think (or perhaps hope, for his sake) that they are exaggerated. But throughout it all, he retains a clear-eyed sense of perspective which I admire, and which keeps his prose from straying into melodrama, as he tells a story I haven't heard before. Well worth the read.

Natalie Haynes
(Judge for the Booker Prize)
Columnist, The Times

A refreshingly honest and candid insight into the private life of a public figure who made a big impression on the local community.

Northwest Mail, Cumbria

A refreshing, down to earth account of the difficulties and challenges facing a Vicar and his family.

Church of England Newspaper

A refreshing read, I couldn't put it down.

Jacqueline Prouse (Sports therapist)

A no-holds-barred, honest, laugh-out-loud funny, sometimes raw autobiography of a Vicar.

Patti Moys (Free Church Minister)

A journey in faith, told with humour, hope and, at times, brutal honesty!

'Tracy Hutchinson' Life Coach

FOREWORD

It is so much easier to learn lessons in life from someone who has run a gauntlet of challenges, temptations, health problems, emotional upheaval, heartache and overwhelming joy - and when that 'someone' is a priest who is charged with the care of our souls as well as our general well-being, the honesty of that message is compelling and personal. This is a book that seesaws the reader from fits of giggles on one page to swirling depths of emotion on the next.

Pam Rhodes
BBC Television Songs of Praise

INTRODUCTION

Can a damaged child with mental health issues and a history of self harm and suicide attempts become a successful priest? Mark Edwards' story of life behind the dog collar is an honest, moving and sometimes hilarious account of a man who is determined to be true his calling, despite a growing conflict with mental health issues arising from a deprived childhood.

The past casts a long shadow over Mark's new life. His first curacy is an unmitigated disaster. A return visit to the children's home he left under a cloud, after a failed suicide attempt as a teenager, reveals that Mark remains scarred by the rejections and turbulent emotions of his childhood.... These insecurities, combined with a serious health problem, lead to misunderstandings with his first training vicar, a siege mentality in the curate's house and a dramatic outburst in the bishop's palace.

Worse still, Mark's once lively faith is beginning to falter as he struggles with his mental health. Unsupported by all except his adored wife Lesley, and a few close friends, Mark retreats behind his role as a parish priest. His dog collar becomes his defence against the world and his battle with his mental health almost leads to breaking point.

'Beyond the Collar' is a deeply honest, humorous book, showing that daily life in the vicarage is subject to mistakes and challenges in the face of pressure from every side; including from within the church itself and not to mention hilarious misunderstandings and fun. But Mark's growing confidence as an Anglican priest masks a deepening crisis, which threatens his vocation, his marriage, his family and his mental well being.

CHAPTER ONE

What was happening to me? One minute I was standing at the altar rail, offering the communion cup to a parishioner, the next minute I blacked out.

Coming round slowly, it took me a while to realise where I was. The outline of the altar rail and a line of pews swam into focus. Then I picked out the concerned face of my new boss, the rector, hovering over me and fussing about as I was helped to my feet. I still felt a bit wobbly, and very embarrassed. I'd made rather an unfortunate spectacle of myself, collapsing right in the middle of taking my first ever service as a newly-ordained deacon and curate in the Church of England.

'Well, you made the headlines,' said my wife, Lesley, coming into my study the following week with the local paper. I thought she was talking about Sunday's service and I was horrified that my collapse had been reported. But I need not have been worried: the headline simply read, 'Furness parish welcomes new curate.' I unfolded the paper across the top of the pile of stuff on my desk and read that I'd settled in well and that everyone at St Mary's in Ulverston, Cumbria, was looking forward to my ministry.

It was only as I studied my photograph alongside the write-up that I realised how sunken my face looked. In fact, I was shocked by my appearance. I could not put it off any longer. I knew I needed to see a doctor.

I had been losing blood from my bowels for weeks. Each time I went to the toilet it looked as though a river of blood had flowed into the pan. Before my ordination in July I had been prescribed some drugs which seemed to clear things up for a while. Recently, however, the bleeding had returned and I was losing weight. I had not been back to see the doctor. There had been so much going on, I simply hadn't had time. We'd had all the packing and unpacking to do as we moved to our new home in Ulverston. Then we needed to find a new school for our children, Jonathan and Fiona. I had been on an ordination retreat at Rose Castle, the home of the Bishop of Carlisle. And there was the excitement of the ordination service itself.

To be honest, though, these were all just excuses. I was scared of what any investigations might reveal. At the back of my mind I thought there was a strong possibility that I might have cancer. I hadn't shared this fear with Lesley. As far as she was concerned, the bleeding had stopped.

*

I winced as the doctor pushed the needle into my vein. I never did like needles.

'Sorry,' he said, 'but I need to take two lots of blood.' I looked out of the window. 'How are you feeling generally? Any unexplained tiredness or other symptoms?'

'Well, yes,' I confessed. 'I feel exhausted. One of my duties is to say Morning Prayer. My boss wants me to do it at 7.30 every day, but sometimes I'm so tired I have to go back to bed afterwards. I'm not trying to skive; I just don't have any energy.'

'OK.' The doctor scribbled a note. 'Anything else you'd like to tell me about?'

'Um,' I didn't like talking about it. 'I bleed when I go to the toilet. Sometimes a lot.'

The doctor listened to all I had to say, then checked my blood pressure.

'It's quite low.' He looked at me over the top of his glasses. 'I'll mark the tests urgent and we should have the results back within 48 hours.'

Lesley's face was a picture of concern as she stood in the hall watching me take the call from the doctor a couple of days later.

His words confirmed my worst suspicions.

'Mark, you need to pack a bag and report immediately to Ward Six at Furness General Hospital. The tests show that your blood count is dangerously low. One big bleed from your back passage and it could be critical. You urgently need a transfusion.'

Despite having only just started my first curacy, I was immediately signed off sick, and began a long round of tests and blood transfusions.

I tried to do a little pastoral visiting, attending the youth club next to the church and generally getting to know people. But the rector and I were already starting to disagree. There had been one incident when I'd asked if I could wear my coloured stole for a baptismal service and he went ballistic. Apparently, the coloured stole is a high church thing, whereas at St Mary's low church traditions were the order of the day. Having been accused of trying to split the church over high and low practices, I retreated to the curate's house, rather taken aback. I was too weak, emotionally and physically, and too young and inexperienced, to stand my ground.

It was still hard to believe that I was not dreaming and that, despite everything, I really was a curate in the Church of England. Only twelve years ago I had been sectioned into a psychiatric hospital, a daunting Victorian building whose corridors echoed with the wailing of its inmates. My childhood experiences in foster homes and in care had left such a painful legacy that I had been on the brink of suicide more than once. Some people, I know, had found me a difficult student, and at one point the bishop had almost withdrawn me from training on health grounds. But at last, having gone through all the rigours of the selection process, studied for four years at university, and undergone a psychiatric assessment to make sure that I was well, I had been ordained in Carlisle Cathedral on July 2, 1995.

I still had a romantic, if not naïve, view of the church and the priesthood. The clergy had always had some kind of mystique, as far as I was concerned. Some clergymen I knew seemed unapproachable and a little scary, but I was determined not to be like that. My calling was strong: I wanted to serve God and serve the people. I wanted to share his love with them and help them grow in their faith. My tutor had said in one of his reports that I would make contacts for the Gospel in unusual places. The flip side to this encouraging remark was that he also issued a warning that my prejudices, frankness and occasional naivety would unsettle some people - a mark, he said, of an authentic vocation, which the church should nurture.

I couldn't argue with the point that I was an unusual man. I'd always resisted conformity and rebelled against those in authority over me. I suspected that the church, with its structure, rituals and hierarchy, would be no different. But, as I saw it, I was in good company. Jesus himself had had little or no time for religious conformity and in the course of his ministry he unsettled the people at the heart of the religious establishment of his day. I was sure he would approve of me, even if others found me difficult.

*

Although I'd only just started my new job, we had a family holiday booked which we were able to take. While we were away we planned to call on my old school buddy Fram, who still lived in Spalding, not far from Ivy Cottage, the children's home where I used to live.

I had mixed feelings about going back. I had left Ivy Cottage under a cloud, after falling in love with Aunty Lindsay, one of the house parents. While I was training for the priesthood, my wife Lesley had suggested that I should meet Lindsay again and confront my infatuation. The reunion with Lindsay almost cost me my vocation as I tried to come to terms with the intense grief of letting go all the strong feelings she had unwittingly engendered in me. I was not sure that I was ready to re-open all those old emotions.

Driving through Lincolnshire, with its flat landscape and fields of tulips, brought back many childhood memories.

Fram insisted that Lesley and the children and I stay the night at his house. It would give us the chance to get to know his American wife, Joel, who we had not met. I was surprised that Fram had married and settled down, but I was even more surprised to discover that he'd got into property and was now running four successful fish and chip shops.

We arrived at Fram's house around dinner time. He came to the door with Joel, who was beautiful. Very tall – and what a figure! Then two toddlers appeared, a boy and a girl, hiding behind Joel's legs. Now that was a surprise – Fram had not said anything about children.

'Amico, how're you doing?' I gave Fram a big hug. He had not changed a bit. 'And it's lovely to meet you, Joel. However did Fram manage to hook such a beautiful girl?' Joel smiled and took Fram's hand. They looked so happy. Maybe revisiting my old haunts would not be so bad.

Jonathon and Fiona were a little shy at first, but within minutes were happily chasing each other round Fram's spacious garden. I felt a bit conscious of my dog collar, which I had chosen to wear for our visit. I think I just wanted to show Fram how much I'd moved on since leaving Spalding as a troubled teenager.

After dinner, Fram and I drove over to see Ivy Cottage. The building was just as I remembered: huge, red brick, its many windows staring out like eyes. Round the back, adjoining the playing fields, the old play room and garages had been redeveloped into a new day centre.

We got out of the car and I walked over to the French doors and peeked in. I could not see anyone around. The room looked pretty much the same, except that the three long tables I remembered had been replaced by smaller, round ones. The only thing that had changed was the new television in the sitting area.

Fram and I walked around the back of the house and I decided to climb the steps of the fire escape up to my old room. Fram followed dutifully. I puffed and panted my way to the top and looked in, expecting to see that nothing had altered. But I saw a small group of boys and girls sitting on a settee watching television. My old bedroom had been transformed into a sitting room.

Alarmed by the sudden appearance of two strange men at the top of the fire escape, a woman dressed in jeans came over immediately and opened the door. She looked very young to me, but it was clear that she was a member of staff.

'Can I help you?'

I explained that I used to live at Ivy Cottage and was visiting for the first time since leaving in 1978.

'Well, in that case, would you like to have a look around?'

I was more than eager, and, stepping into my old room, felt that I was immediately transported back in time. Memories of my stay at the home came flooding back. I could see the rest of the boys - Gary, Richard, my brother Paul - all squabbling over something or other. I could see my bed, clear as day. And then – yes - there was Aunty Lindsay, at that time the love of my life. Tears welled up as I remembered the struggle she had to try and break down my tough, protective shell and show some kindness to the lonely little boy inside.

Further memories flashed across my mind as I stood beside the fire door. Memories of Aunty Lindsay wrestling the scalpel blade out of my hand as I tried to cut my wrists and end the torture of all my conflicting emotions. Sixteen years had passed but here I was again, the feelings still fresh and painful.

'Are you OK, Mark?' Fram put a comforting hand on my shoulder.

'I'll be fine, I just need a minute.' I tried to ignore the children sniggering on the settee.

Fram and I followed the house-parent out of the room into the long corridor. At once, in my mind's eye, I could picture Aunty Freda telling some boy off and threatening him with a slipper across his bottom if he did not get back into bed straight away.

Opening the door to what had been the boys' bathroom, I relived the moment when Aunty Lindsay had first arrived at Ivy Cottage and I had to have my first bath under her supervision. I was fifteen and she was twenty-four but the old fashioned regime of bath time supervision was still practised in 1977. These days it would simply never be allowed. Mind you, Aunty Lindsay was always very discreet and never stood over us, watching, like some of the older house parents did.

Moving on down the corridor, we went past Aunty Lindsay's old room. I was beginning to think that coming back had been a bad idea. I knew that I had treated Aunty Lindsay badly. There had been a time when I had wanted her to punish me, to prove her love for me. That might sound weird, but I had been so starved of love and affection as a child that I would have welcomed discipline as evidence that someone cared for me enough to want to correct me. If truth be told, I pushed and pushed Aunty Lindsay to the point when I really thought she would spank me. She never did. But I often wondered how I would have felt if she had.

I could not turn back the clock and put things right, or pretend they'd never happened. Here I was, in the present, and I didn't much like what I was seeing. The new regime was much more relaxed than in my day, too much so, if you asked me. Children were jumping on the furniture, smoking, being disrespectful and using language that was colourful, to say the least. In my day we never got away with behaviour like that. I was once spanked by Aunty Freda for swearing. I haven't sworn again, to this day. Yes, some of the old regime did need to change, but this looked like a free-for-all to me.

'The kids know we can't touch them,' the house parent explained, seeing my reactions to what was going on around us. 'But some of them do need a smack.'

I agreed. I felt grateful that, when I was there at least, we felt secure within a regime which had strict boundaries we knew we must not cross. I had lived at Ivy Cottage for seven years, longer than I had been anywhere else, and it was the only home I really knew.

Driving back to Fram's house, tears ran down my cheeks. For the rest of the evening my spirits were sombre, but it was good to talk to Fram and Joel and to reminisce about our time together at Westlode Infants and Gleed Boys Secondary School. Yes, my childhood had been far from perfect but there had been good times despite everything.

It was time to leave the past behind and move on. As we left Fram and Joel's house to finish our holiday I had no idea that my health was to take an unexpected turn and my career in the church would hang in the balance.

*

February 1996 was a terrible month. For a start, it was one of the worst winters on record since the 1940s. I was on a clergy retreat along with the rector and other local clergy and we ended up being trapped at the retreat centre, cut off by the snow. The long, narrow, winding road back home to Ulverston was virtually impassable.

The last thing I wanted was to be stuck with the rector for another day, as the relationship between us was really breaking down. I knew that he believed my collapse and my health problems were all down to stress and I simply wasn't up to the job. He thought I was unfit to be a priest.

I wished he'd just go home and leave me to it, but he insisted that we both get a lift with another vicar whose 4 x 4 vehicle could cope with the difficult conditions on the roads.

It was the most uncomfortable drive I think I've ever had. The rector did not say a word for the whole of the two hour journey – one which would normally take 45 minutes. I avoided eye contact with him, looking out instead at the cars and buses abandoned in ditches and beside the road, and wishing I was safely home.

Finally we arrived, and the rector broke his silence to tell me to be at the rectory at seven o'clock. By the time I had waded through yet another fresh snow fall it was 7.30, and when he opened the door to me I could see that he was boiling with fury. He demanded to know how much longer I was going to be off sick.

I had no answer to that question. The hospital was still conducting all manner of tests but had not been able to find out why I was losing so much blood. Regular transfusions were keeping me going, but that could not go on indefinitely. They had to find the root cause.

Lesley and I were feeling isolated and vulnerable, mostly because we couldn't share with anyone in the church what was happening. How could I come out and say that I was being bullied by the rector, as well as being ill? I did not think anyone would believe me. I was still very young, both in age and in emotional development, and I found it really difficult to cope with feeling rejected again. It was not just the weather that was hemming me in, I felt as though I was under siege in the curate's house.

The day before I was due to go back into hospital for another transfusion, I decided to call my old tutor, John Pritchard. During our chat he warned me that he sensed the rector might be about to sack me.

The minute I put the phone down, I ran round to the rectory and banged on the door. After a few minutes it was opened a fraction and I saw the rector's face peering out.

'I've just been speaking to John Pritchard. He says I should talk to you,' I began.

I desperately needed to know what was going on. My career – well, it was more than a career, it was my vocation – and my family's future were at stake.

'I can't talk to you now. You'll be hearing from the bishop soon.' With that, the rector slammed the door. I was left standing on the step with a growing sense of foreboding.

Whatever the bishop had to say to me had to wait, however?

I was admitted to Ward Six of Furness General Hospital, into the care of lovely Sister Olive, and had yet another blood transfusion and more tests.

I tried to read the consultant's expression as he approached my bed, but he was too calm and professional to give anything away.

'Mark, the results aren't entirely clear.' My stomach lurched and my hands felt sweaty.

'You should prepare yourself for the possibility that you might have cancer.'

It frightening to hear the Big C mentioned like that, out in the open for the first time. I already knew that it might be a possibility, but I'd tried to keep the idea firmly at the back of my mind. Despite the funerals I'd conducted as a newly-ordained curate, I hadn't really faced up to my own mortality until now. I was kept in hospital for a week.

During my stay, Gerald Garbutte, the hospital chaplain, visited me often and I began to share with him a little of what was happening to me outside the ward. Gerald had no time for the church establishment: as a gay priest he'd encountered more than his fair share of bigotry and prejudice and he'd become disillusioned. Over the next few years, Gerald and I became good friends. As my spiritual director, he became the person I could talk to when I wanted to let off steam or pour my heart out. I learnt to share with Gerald things I'd never dare mention to colleagues or superiors.

*

A few days after leaving hospital, I received a letter from the bishop's office, inviting me and Lesley to Rose Castle to talk to him. I was pleased to have the opportunity – Gerald had advised me that I should talk to the bishop as soon as I was fit enough – but my stomach went into overdrive with butterflies for days before the visit. I'd always had a problem with authority figures and bishops were no exception. I knew that whatever happened I was at his mercy.

'Welcome, Mark. Welcome, Lesley.' Bishop Ian smiled reassuringly as he led us into his study. Rose Castle was small by castle standards, but still large enough to be intimidating. My last visit there had been nine months earlier, as one of a group of ordinands preparing to take our vows, when we had all listened to the bishop talk about vocation and the priesthood. Little did I realise then that I had to be back so soon, with my future as a priest hanging in the balance.

Lesley and I sat in two slippery leather chairs facing the bishop, who settled himself behind a large desk.

We waited.

'It's been a choppy nine months, for you, hasn't it, Mark?' the bishop said. 'Would you like to explain, in your own words, what's been going on?'

The whole scene was uncomfortably like the times in the children's home when I was called in to the superintendent's office to give an account of myself. Here I was again, still having to explain myself to someone who had ultimate power and control over my destiny. It was not a good feeling.

I exploded.

I let rip for a good twenty minutes, as months of suppressed pain and anger came boiling up to the surface. The bishop sat in stunned silence as I rose from my chair and did my best Hitler impression, waving my arms about, slamming my fist down on the desk and demanding that action be taken against the rector.

The bishop let me carry on until I had run out of steam and flopped back into my chair, exhausted.

There was silence for a moment.

'Could I just bring Lesley in at this point?' the bishop suggested calmly.

'Lesley,' I thought, 'Oh…' I'd completely lost sight of the fact that she was sitting beside me; I'd been so blinded by a red mist of fury. 'Oh yes, please, do let's bring Lesley in.'

My lovely wife, she was always the voice of reason in our marriage. Self-controlled and loving, she always stuck by me, whatever the provocation or upset. There had been times when I'd tried to physically push her out of the door, telling her that I was no good for her and she'd be better off leaving me. But she never did. I felt that she demonstrated an inner strength that was beyond explanation: she put it down to her stable upbringing. I could only envy the qualities which made her such a beautiful person and wonderful wife.

I remembered the day when I had announced to my pastor at Chester City Mission that Lesley and I were going out. I was sure he'd be thrilled that I'd found such a lovely girlfriend. But I soon discovered that he'd already spent almost two hours trying to persuade her not to go out with me. He went on and on about how unsuitable we were for each other.

'Look, Mark, be reasonable.' He looked me straight in the eye. 'You spent your whole childhood in and out of care. You've tried to commit suicide three times. You've been in and out of the mental hospital for most of the last six months. You've got no qualifications whatsoever, and frankly you've got no prospects.'

And, as if to hammer home the differences between us, he concluded by reminding me that Lesley had just graduated from university and was the pride and joy of her nice middle class parents.

'So what's your point?' My voice sounded angry with disappointment.

'My point is, this relationship is unworkable. And I doubt that Lesley's parents will ever accept you.'

Later, when he married us at Chester City Mission in 1984, that same pastor cheerfully admitted that he'd been wrong. And as for Lesley's parents, they may have hoped for someone with better prospects to marry their daughter, but they accepted me, without prejudice and without judgment. They never said a word against me, not even when, just a week before our wedding, we had nowhere to live except my tiny bed-sit. Over the years, they were able to become proud of me. And I was equally proud to call them my in-laws, having finally learnt to put my working-class prejudices behind me.

But now, back in the bishop's palace, it was time for my wife to speak.

Lesley shared her own pain and sense of isolation.

'It's even more difficult,' she concluded, 'because we don't feel it's right to talk to anyone, so no one knows what's really going on. And we're so worried about Mark's health. The doctors say that he might have cancer, and he'll probably need surgery.'

The bishop was sympathetic and expressed his support and concern for us as a family.

Then the room fell silent.

Resting his chin on his hands, the bishop gave me the news that I'd been expecting all along. The rector no longer wanted to work with me and was giving me the sack.

I was too stunned to respond. Lesley reached out her hand and grasped mine. I tried hard to concentrate as the bishop explained that he was not suspending me or taking away my license, but he had to acknowledge the fact that my curacy had not worked out.

'It's not a reflection on you, Mark,' he said, standing up. The interview was over. 'It's just an unfortunate conflict of personalities. Sometimes this sort of thing does happen.'

I felt just like I had felt when I had been told to pack my bags and leave Ivy Cottage because of my adolescent crush on Aunty Lindsay. I was being rejected again, and it hurt.

CHAPTER TWO

The following weeks were not easy.

As the curate's house was just across the road from the church, it was inevitable that church members would knock on the door and ask how I was getting on. But we couldn't tell them – the bishop had asked us not to. He had promised to re-start my curacy elsewhere, but my ordination to the office of priest would have to be postponed for a year. It felt so unfair: I'd had to do an extra year at university in order to prove myself, and now I was having to start at the beginning all over again.

The emotional turmoil I felt was making me snappy and angry. But I was also so physically weak that some days I couldn't stand up long enough to have a shower and had to lie down on the bathroom floor.

Eventually, Lesley and I had had enough of deceiving people. We decided to share what was going on with a few of our closest friends. They were shocked and upset, and one of them, a retired policeman, wanted to go round straight away and have it out with the rector. It took all our powers of persuasion to calm him down.

Naturally, within the parish, opinions were divided as to the rights and wrongs of it all. As you would expect, some remained loyal to the rector, some felt like piggy in the middle and a small group supported us as best they could.

In early July, I went under the surgeon's knife. The cause of my bleeding had finally been diagnosed as a large intestinal diverticulum which needed to be removed. I was in surgery for three hours and when I came round I was told that the operation had been a success. Part of my bowel had been removed and my appendix had been taken out. And the good news was there were no traces of cancer and I was expected to make a full recovery.

After a three week holiday down south I started to look towards the future and think seriously about myself and about my calling. To be honest, my state of mind could be summed up as, 'stuff the church, I'll take my chances with the heathen!'

The stress of my illness and the problems with my curacy meant that a lot of unresolved anger from my past had surfaced into the present. Although I was learning to play a professional role as a clergyman, behind closed doors my inner child still dominated my personality. My own children got used to witnessing outbursts of anger and random acts of violence towards inanimate objects as my temper got the better of me. The sudden thump of my foot against a door would reverberate through the apparent tranquillity of the curate's house. I could not help it – I felt so frustrated and insecure when faced with situations I couldn't control.

For a long time I'd felt as though I had a split personality. The truth was, I did. Despite the healing I'd already received for my troubled and abusive childhood, I was still immature. Part of me was trapped in a time warp. But I did understand a little about psychology, having studied the subject, and had a certain amount of self awareness about why I reacted in the way I did to trigger events.

I hoped that, through my faith in him, God would bring me to the point where I was truly free from the baggage of the past. But I knew that spiritual healing didn't happen overnight. It was a process of letting go and allowing God access to the painful areas.

And perhaps, if I'm honest, being the victim had become such a way of life for me that subconsciously I'd come to need the drama and the crises. Victims feel powerless and weak and part of them loves that, because it means that they don't have to do anything or take responsibility for their actions. They feel persecuted and picked on and wallow in their suffering. Being a victim can give you an identity: it's better to be a victim that to be a nobody. I was starting to feel like that.

But throughout the difficult times, Lesley never once condemned or judged me. She understood that my inner child was still hurting, still vulnerable and still needing reassurance. She ministered to me, prayed for me and reminded me just how much I was loved by her and by God. Deep down, though, she longed for the day when I would be free from my past and able to be all that God intended me to be.

What I really wanted was to be myself and let Christ shine through my personality, not in spite of it. I accepted that things should be done in a dignified and orderly fashion in church, but surely God didn't mind how I spoke, or how I stood, or what gestures I made from the pulpit. And surely people outside the church needed to see a human being behind the dog collar, not some falsely perfect mechanical toy.

I hated the idea of being squeezed into a 'holy' mould. I'd seen it happen at theological college: students who were talking to you normally would suddenly break into a special pious voice as they invited the assembly to worship. It was like one of those dolls with a cord at the back of their heads which you pull to get them to talk. If only I could master that special holy voice, I thought, I'd be accepted. But there was no way I wanted to become a robot.

I made a bargain with God.

'Lord, I give you three months to turn things around,' I prayed. 'Otherwise I'll resign from holy orders.' Three months seemed as good a time as any.

They were just coming to an end when a letter arrived from the bishop's office. My hands shook as I opened it. But it was good news. The bishop was formally inviting me to re-start my curacy under the Reverend Ian Davis at St John's, Barrow Island.

*

The first time I met Ian Davis and his wife Sheila I was defensive and guarded. My experience with the rector had reinforced my childhood view of people: trust no one. Especially, don't trust anyone who tells you to trust them – they're the people you really have to watch.

Lesley and I were invited to Ian and Sheila's house for a visit. Sensing our unease, Ian sat on the floor and talked about football, always a good place to start if you both support Manchester United! Sheila was more interested in finding out about the children and she chatted separately to Lesley.

It didn't take me long to drop my guard. And once I got started I couldn't stop pouring out all the pain and anger I felt about what seemed to me to be another rejection. Not just of me personally, but my whole family.

As I struggled with an overwhelming tide of emotion, something unexpected happened.

Prompted by the Holy Spirit, Ian got up off the floor, Sheila out of her chair, and they both came and sat either side of us. They reached out their arms to grasp one another, with Lesley and me in the middle, and just held us. At that moment we felt such warmth and such love coming from them that we both broke down and cried.

When we became quiet, Ian prayed, asking God to fill us with his love and peace, to bring us healing and to bless our family.

After all that we'd been through, just to be held by someone and feel God's love pouring through them gave us a strong feeling that from now on things were going to get better. Sometimes you really do need 'God with skin on' - the ministry of healing through touch.

After that first meeting with Ian and Sheila, events moved quickly. The bishop wanted me launched back into ministry as soon as possible. There were the inevitable formalities and practical issues to be sorted out. St John's was not a large church and the congregation wouldn't be able to pay my expenses, so it was agreed that I would be funded by the diocese. And until a curate's house was purchased, we'd carry on living in the curate's house in Ulverston, eight miles from Barrow Island.

My priesting was to be delayed for at least another year and I would only be ordained once I'd completed a full uninterrupted year as a curate and the bishop had received a positive report from Ian. I knew I'd have to work hard to prove that I was a suitable candidate to be an Anglican priest. I suspected – rightly, as it turned out – that I already had a reputation as a problem curate.

Little did I realise what a great partnership Ian and I would turn out to be.

I was licensed and received my new orders during the Christingle service at St John's on Sunday 15 December. Once again, my family was there to watch with pride. I felt positive about my future in the Church. I knew that things would get better and the difficulties and traumas of the last year would soon fade, although I also realised that it would take me some while to forgive and let go of the sense of betrayal I was still feeling. But all I wanted was to serve God as a humble parish priest. As far as I was concerned, there was no higher calling.

Jonathan and Fiona might not have understood the full significance of my special service but they did know that Daddy had a new church and he was happy again. After the service they ran round the back, chasing each other and trying to pinch the sweets from the Christingle oranges. No one minded, least of all Ian the vicar. It was the kind of church where children were welcomed. We'd only been there a short time but already we felt at home.

*

It was every parent's nightmare.

Fiona's terrified voice on the phone: 'Dad! I've been kidnapped!'

I froze, panic rising inside.

'Where are you? What's happened?'

'We were at the shops. He made us get into his car!'

'Where are you now?'

'The phone box. Just outside Ulverston. He panicked and let us go!'

'Don't move – I'm coming to get you!' I thrust the phone at Lesley, who was standing right beside me, told her to ring the police, and raced out to the car.

I could not think straight. What if the man went back and forced Fiona and her friend to get into his car again? I had to get there as quickly as possible! I jumped two sets of red lights, daring any police officer to pull me over as I rushed to my daughter's rescue. Within minutes I was in sight of the phone box. I could see the girls standing there. Pulling alongside, I wound down the window.

'Quick! Get in!'

I was furious that Fiona had gone into town without permission, but I was trembling with relief that she and her friend were safe. Fiona repeated her story about being forced into a car by a man they'd seen at the shops. But something wasn't quite right.

I looked at them both in the rear view mirror. Neither of them seemed too distressed, considering the ordeal they'd just been through. I didn't give myself time to think, though. I just did a U-turn and drove back into town, screeching to a halt in the forecourt of Ulverston police station.

Getting out of the car, still shaking with shock, I saw a police officer about to climb into his own vehicle. He could see that I was in a state.

'Hello, sir. Is there a problem?'

'There certainly is! My eight-year-old daughter and her friend have just been forced into a car by a man and driven half-way out of town!'

The police officer was immediately concerned. He invited the girls to get out of the car and follow him into the police station. Once inside, he asked a WPC to join him and the girls in the interview room, while I waited outside, reliving what had just happened and trying to stop shaking.

It seemed ages before the police officer reappeared. When he did, I sprang out of my seat.

'You may wish to remain seated, sir.'

'Why? What have they told you?' All my panic returned in a rush. 'What's happened? Have they been abused? What have they said?' I thought I was going to pass out. And then I realised: 'I'm sorry! I'm a clergyman, I should be able to stay calm in a crisis.'

'I don't doubt your vocation.' The officer rested his hand gently on my shoulder. 'You may be a clergyman but you're also a father. I have to tell you that your daughter and her friend have made up the whole story.'

I looked at him and opened my mouth to speak, but nothing came out. I gulped and tried again.

'I'm sorry, I think I must be in shock. I thought I heard you say that those girls made everything up.'

The officer nodded. They thought they'd get into trouble for wandering down to the shops without permission. Hence the kidnap story…

I was on my feet, shouting again.

'Where is she? I've just jumped two red lights! My wife is at home, beside herself with worry! Just wait till I get that young lady home!'

The girls were very quiet as I drove off. After dropping Fiona's friend at her house, making it abundantly clear to her father what had happened and suggesting that he disciplined his daughter as I intended to discipline Fiona, we got back to the curate's house. As soon as we were through the door I shouted to Lesley that they were all right but they'd made the whole thing up. Dragging Fiona by the hand behind me, I sat down on the nearest chair and flung her over my knee. She felt every blow and I meant every one.

How dare she put us through such worry!

How dare she lie to me!

How dare she wander off!

Lesley and I had always smacked our children when we considered it necessary, which wasn't very often. I was incensed by the anti-smacking lobby: no one had any right to tell me as a parent how to bring up my children. Over the years, I would campaign and defend the rights of children to be protected from abuse. I'd been abused as a child myself, and I knew full well the huge difference between a blow harsh enough to cause bruising, cuts and lasting marks, and a smack on the bottom delivered in the context of a loving and caring environment. I'd been beaten by some of my foster parents and still bore the emotional scars. In contrast, I'd been smacked for bad behaviour in the children's home, and each time I'd richly deserved it. It has always amazed and angered me that good parents, who attempt to lay down a clear moral framework for their children and enforce boundaries by smacking, can be taken to task by the authorities, but no one seems to care about parents who verbally abuse their children. This, I believe from bitter experience, has a far more lasting effect on a child's emotional and psychological development than a smack by a loving parent. I would never do anything to hurt my children or undermine their dignity as human beings.

Within an hour, the whole kidnap incident was forgotten and Fiona and I were playing and laughing together in the garden.

*

Ian was just what I needed in a training vicar. He loved me like a son and wasn't afraid to speak his mind and rebuke me if I needed it. He was also quick to praise and affirm me.

The first time I preached, before I'd even stepped down from the pulpit, he addressed the congregation and said I'd preached a great sermon. Hearing that public affirmation, and the round of applause that followed, meant the world to me. Everyone in the parish who saw us working together said what a good team we made.

There were a couple of times when Ian had to put me straight on issues which could have got out of hand. The first time, he called me into his study.

'There's a rumour going round about you, Mark,' he said. 'People say that you've been seen going into a massage parlour.'

I felt sick. How could people be so narrow minded?

What I was actually doing was going for remedial aromatherapy, which my GP had recommended to unlock stress-related spasms in my back. I enjoyed the aromatherapy sessions – they were relaxing, as well as helping my back problems.

But I could see that, although it was perfectly innocent and I was going with Lesley's full knowledge and approval, my visits might give the appearance of evil. Ian was concerned about his curate being on the wrong end of smutty talk, so I cancelled the rest of my appointments.

The second time Ian had to pull me up was when I got a computer. It's difficult to explain now, because technology is so much part of our lives that we can't imagine what it was like without computers, but when I first got mine I was completely fascinated by it. In awe of it, really. I was like a kid with a new toy and couldn't get over the excitement of seeing email ping into my inbox. I couldn't tear myself away from the wretched thing and started spending more time with my computer than out in the parish with my parishoners.

Eventually I heard from a distant cousin who emailed from America, sending me photographs of herself and her family.

'Isn't this great?' I said to Lesley, showing her the pictures. 'I've got a pen friend in America!'

I was so impressed that I printed off a picture and took it round to the vicarage to show Ian.

'You idiot!' He wagged his finger at me, much to my surprise. 'Don't you understand how dangerous email relationships can be?'

His warning fell on deaf ears. I thought he was an old fuddy duddy. And anyway, what right did he have to tell me what to do? I sulked for a few days, like a spoilt teenager.

How I wish I'd listened to him.

This lady turned out to be an internet stalker. At first I got a bit carried away with the banter we exchanged. It was just a laugh and a joke – and maybe some mild flirting. But it soon went sour. Although I tried to keep things friendly and the conversation above board, she got mad as hell. As time went on, I realised what a fool I'd been. It got really scary and I had visions of her coming over to England to bump off Lesley so that she could have me all to herself. I was convinced that I was a marked man. I could not shake off a mental image of myself tied to the bed having both legs broken with a sledge-hammer, like in the film *Misery* starring Kathy Bates.

Eventually a friend showed me how to block and change my email, and I never heard from that woman again.

I still had teething problems with the new technology, though. Once I accidentally put a pornographic image on my desk top. This was in the days before spam blockers and virus protection, and I had no idea how the image even got onto my computer. Lesley was in hysterics when she saw it and nearly wet herself laughing.

Life as Ian's curate was not all struggling with computers and parish work, however. He and I played squash together regularly. It was frustrating because he always beat me, despite being ten years my senior and overweight. And once he and I had started attending the local aerobics class together, it was even worse – the svelte, slim-line Ian was even faster on the squash court!

On one particular occasion I'd just had a row with my son, Jonathan, and arrived at the squash court already in a temper. I got so angry when I lost again that I let go of my racket and nearly took Ian's head off.

'What the hell do you think you're doing?' He was not amused.

'It's Jonathan,' I fumed. 'He's just like my brother.'

With that, Ian pinned me against the wall with his right arm, shaking his left fist in my face.

'He's not like your brother! He's like you! It's time you learnt to get a grip on your temper!' Ian proceeded to give me a lecture about what it would be like once I had my own parish. Lots of people would wind me up, especially at church council meetings, which were often full of people with their own agendas, playing one off against each other. What would I do then? I'd be the person responsible for keeping order and discipline. And I should be demonstrating God's love! Which I could hardly do if I got involved in a fight, could I?

'Imagine the headlines: "Vicar thumps church warden in argument about hymn books"! Come on Mark, you'll get into serious trouble if you don't master your anger. And you'll probably end up having a stroke before you're forty!'

I was so relieved when he let go of me – his elbow had been obstructing my windpipe!

He was right, though. It was not just on the squash court that my anger got the better of me. Usually it was little things that triggered an outburst. The house being untidy, or the kids squabbling, or Lesley having forgotten to pass on an important message. It was not constant: I could go a long time without even raising my voice, but then something or someone would upset me and I'd just lose it.

I wished I could do more to control my temper. Sometimes I scared myself as well as my family, and I always felt so guilty after an explosion of anger.

Lesley was the exact opposite of me: nothing ever seemed to upset or rattle her. She was calm, sane and rational the whole time.

'Come on, level with me,' I'd say to her. 'Are you an angel in human form?' At times she seemed too good to be true, and I wondered whether she'd make the better priest. She was certainly the better Christian.

*

I could hardly believe what I was reading. After only ten months as Ian's curate, he had written a report to the bishop requesting that I should be ordained priest.

'Since joining me,' Ian wrote, 'Mark has shown himself willing to give himself fully to every task and challenge set before him. He is diligent in parish visiting and is spoken highly of by those he visits. He also takes extended communion to the house-bound, which he enjoys as much as they do. He is involved in the local primary and secondary schools, where he helps with after-school clubs. He shadows me in other activities where he is not so confident, or where I am in a role that is not yet required of him. He constantly asks questions about all that we do together, which is a very positive means of development for him.

'We meet together regularly for daily prayer and to plan and discuss. I find myself able to give him a plan of what needs doing in the coming weeks, knowing that Mark will get on with it. He assists me in all the services, by his own choice, and has taken funerals and baptisms as well as baptism preparation. He thrives on praise, and has responded well to the continuing welcome that he receives in the church and parish. Lesley and Sheila also get on well together and are proving a mutual source of help and support.

'Mark is maturing in ministry and has lost a lot of his brashness. He is inclined to count to ten and decide not to leap into a situation until he has checked how deep it is. I find him an encouragement to my own ministry and have come to view him as a valued colleague on whom I can rely. He will make a fine priest. He has a real love for the people and a real passion for the Gospel.

'I respectfully ask that due consideration be given to Mark being ordained priest at Michaelmas. I am certain that he is ready for this further step forward in his growing and maturing ministry.'

I read it again. Was this really me, the problem curate? Perhaps Ian had made a mistake. I did not feel at all confident, but I knew that the last ten months had been a positive experience, especially compared to my previous, aborted curacy.

I was beginning to feel more at ease wearing my dog collar. Seeing someone sporting a clerical collar can have a strange effect on people, I'd discovered. For most people within the church, my collar was a symbol of my office, and I was shown great respect when I was wearing it. For a minority in any parish, however, the church is merely a power base and they have no time for the clergy. These people are almost never committed Christians who love the Lord – they're more like the religious people of Jesus' day who he condemned as hypocrites. They're more interested in hanging on to their traditions and rituals than caring for the lost.

Once, all hell broke loose in the vestry after a service when outsiders had dared to approach the communion rail to take the sacrament. Some of them were so aware of their own shortcomings that they could barely look me in the eye as they took the bread and drank the wine. Unlike some of the regular church goers, who were infuriated by their presence. I have sometimes had to give communion to people who, if looks could kill, would have cheerfully seen me dead on the carpet before they got back to their seats. I don't know how they can square such behaviour with the teaching of Christ, which instructs us to be reconciled to our brothers and sisters before taking the bread and wine lest we eat and drink judgment on ourselves.

Yes, I'm as guilty as the next man of being too quick to pass judgment, but as I grew in faith I became quicker to repent. It isn't my place to ask people for their credentials before taking communion – after all, it is a sacrament of grace. And I have been privileged to know many good people who would have walked over hot coals for me as their vicar, and who sincerely respected my office as priest.

For those outside the church, the dog collar can have really strange effects. Some people ignore it completely, obviously hoping that I will go away. Others immediately engage me in conversation, explaining how they used to go to church, or used to be in the choir, or are not very religious. Or they'll tell me that they have a distant cousin twice removed who had an uncle who had a nephew whose sister married a vicar who ran off with the organist, but he's dead now…

'Oh, really?' I'd say. 'Isn't that wonderful … super … smashing …' Lesley used to get so embarrassed standing next to me as I went through my 'wonderful, super, smashing,' routine.

I did feel that I had to watch how I behaved in public when I was wearing the collar. I suppose that's not a bad thing: I was effectively wearing a uniform identifying me as a man of God, so my behaviour should reflect that. That's not to say I can't be real with people or less than human. Some people say that the collar is a barrier and it alienates people. That's not been my experience – I think it's a lack of personality and humanity that alienates, not wearing a small white collar. To be honest, I like watching peoples' reactions when I'm wearing the collar, especially when I'm out with Lesley and she looks particularly sexy and hot. Once she and I were having lunch in Morrisons, and she had on a really hugging dress which left little to the imagination, and a sexy pair of boots. I noticed all the men ogling her. Some did a double take when they realised she was with the vicar!

Collar or not, I felt good leaving the vicarage clutching a copy of Ian's report about me. I was glad God had turned things around for me and I hadn't had to leave the church. I was enjoying every minute of my ministry.

*

'Curate's big day finally arrives,' reported the local paper. On Sunday 28 September 1997 I was ordained priest in Carlisle Cathedral. It was a proud moment for me and my family – and a day I'd thought would never arrive. I had finally proved to everyone that I did have what it takes to become a priest. I was very aware of how far I'd come since my troubled childhood and the pain and isolation of my adolescence.

But I knew that I still carried with me some of that pain and those troubled emotions. The difference was, I now had a role to hide behind. As long as I committed myself to helping others, I wouldn't have to confront my own problems or the unresolved issues from my past.

Well, that's what I thought. But God had other plans. Over the years, he slowly stripped away the veneer until it was just me and him.

My own church history had been a somewhat chequered one. During my seven years at Ivy Cottage, the children's home, we all went to church every Sunday, trooping down the road in a long crocodile to the local Methodist chapel. I found the whole thing boring – I'd rather have been out playing and getting up to mischief. We were all a bit disruptive, despite the threat of a belting from Uncle Andrews, the superintendent of the home.

One Sunday, a fight broke out in the upper rooms of the Methodist church and some furniture got broken. After that, the four main protagonists – including me and my brother Paul – were told we were no longer welcome there. Paul and I were sent to the local Baptist church instead.

I enjoyed the services there more, and got involved with the Boys' Brigade. I didn't have much time for all the Bible bashing though. Sunday school was OK, and so were the Sunday school outings, but I was always causing trouble, playing the clown and trying to shock. Once, I made a huge penis out of plasticine and stuck it onto a Sunday school model of some character from the Bible. The boys were delighted – the girls just screamed!

I carried on going to the Baptist church long after it ceased to be compulsory, right up until the time I left Ivy Cottage. There was a real warmth to the people I met there and they made me feel part of the church family. I still didn't understand what it was to make a personal commitment to Christ, but overall my experience of church had been positive.

Now, after my ordination as priest, I found that my ministry became wider than when I was a curate, and I was able to reach more people. I was allowed to baptize children, give the blessing, celebrate the Mass and marry couples. Ian started to take more of a back seat and allow me room to develop without watching me the whole time. I was finally starting to grow in confidence – and people noticed the change.

'You were like a scared rabbit at first,' said Betty the church warden one day, giving me a big hug. She was a dear lady and liked to mother me – and box my ears if I needed it! You didn't mess with Betty, she ran the church and ran it well.

Ian told me he was proud of me. But despite everything, – my growing reputation from Barrow to Carlisle, my greater experience in ministry and my genuinely collaborative partnership with Ian Davies – underneath it all I still believed that everyone else was better than me. Lesley hated it when I put myself down, saying that I wasn't a proper vicar and wishing I could be more like my colleagues. She did not want to be known as the vicar's wife, she had the confidence to be her own person. As well as being mother to two growing children, she was pursuing her own career, working with people with learning disabilities and earning a good salary. She had made many sacrifices so that I could follow my calling, but, more than that, she complemented me exactly and gave me the stability and love I'd never had as a child.

CHAPTER THREE

Then, just as I was starting to feel I was making headway, my past came rushing back when I least expected it.

Before we left Barrow for our annual holiday down south, I'd had a call from my sister Shene, saying that our mother was not well and had been taken into hospital. I'd never had the chance to bond with my mother, so the news did not really bother me.

I'd last seen my mother before I was first ordained, when we'd dragged the children over to see her in Boston.

Our visit was memorable for all the wrong reasons. The house was filthy, with empty alcohol bottles scattered everywhere, and it smelt bad. Old newspapers, piles of them, were stacked up on one side of the room. Cats roamed around, sleeping wherever they could find a space. My mother looked unkempt in an old nylon overall held together with a piece of string.

I felt sorry for Lesley and the children, who were perched on one end of the worn-out settee. They could not sit back and relax because of the cats.

I tried to make conversation, but it was difficult, and there were long periods of silence.

It was the first time that my mother had seen me in my dog collar. I wore it especially to show her that I had done something with my life. I had hoped she'd feel proud of me. I guess she did: she dragged me round the cul de sac to show me off to her neighbours.

'This is my boy, the priest,' she announced to anyone who saw us. She was obviously drunk and kept slurring her words. I was embarrassed to be seen with her. Although I called her mum, she was really a complete stranger. All she'd ever done for me was give birth to me. She'd certainly played no part in my success. When I was sectioned onto the psychiatric wing after having tried to take my own life, she did not want to know.

I only went to see her that day because I was desperate for some kind of acknowledgment from her that I'd done well and she was proud of me.

Lesley could see I was upset when we left.

The kids could not wait to leg it out of the house. They kept going on and on about how the house stank and how grandma had tried to kiss them with her horrible lips. She'd tried to kiss me too, but one whiff of her breath and I'd turned away.

And now she was in hospital. What was I supposed to do?

We set off on holiday as normal and had a good time. The children enjoyed the beach and the other attractions. I didn't feel all that concerned about my mother, but coming back from a visit to the Army museum I had a sudden attack of conscience. Jonathan and Fiona were messing about in the back of the car. I pulled over at the next telephone kiosk and decided to call the hospital.

'Hold on a moment,' said the nurse who answered. I could tell from her voice that something was wrong. 'I'll just get the doctor for you,' she continued.

'I'm very sorry, Reverend Edwards.' The doctor's hushed tones confirmed my sudden fear. 'Your mother has just died.'

At that moment, I did not know what to feel. I simply said, 'Thank you doctor. I appreciate you telling me,' and put the phone down. I stood by myself in the telephone box for a moment and started to cry. Looking out towards the car, I could see Lesley kneeling in her seat facing back towards the kids and smacking them on the legs. Composing myself, I walked over to the car and got in.

'How is she?' Lesley asked.

'Oh Les, she's just died.' Tears began to well up again. Jonathan and Fiona were still fighting – I don't think they'd even heard what I said.

Lesley snapped round to face them again.

'Stop it! Your Dad's Mum has just died. Behave yourselves!' She never normally raised her voice to the kids so shouting at them did the trick – they shut up.

Lesley put her arms round me to comfort me. I just cried and cried. I don't know why.

For days afterwards, all I could think about was the past. I kept replaying it in my mind, over and over again. I particularly remembered the moment when I was taken from my mother's arms into care when I was three. All the negative emotions from my childhood came surging back into the present. I was hurting so badly. I hated my mother and all the people I felt had screwed up my childhood. I couldn't reconcile any of these emotions with my faith or my vocation.

I'd received a lot of healing over the years, but had I really dealt with my past? Or had I just learnt to live with it? How could I forgive?

God was challenging me to let go. It was as if Jesus was asking me the same question he asked the cripple lying by the pool. A man who made his living from begging; a man who had suffered for years, who had become comfortable with his condition. 'Do you want to be well?' Jesus asked him.

Over the course of my ministry I would counsel many people who didn't really want to get well. Like me, they didn't really want to let go of the past because, like me, they needed to be a victim. But, as I was to discover in my own journey, it's impossible to move forward until you do let go.

For the time being I was on a downward spiral of self absorption. The question I kept asking myself was, how could my parents have let us suffer so much as children?

I tried to enjoy the rest of the holiday but I could not. I heard later that my mother shouted out my name as she was dying. I felt I should have been there. As a priest I could at least have given her the last rites.

*

'What have you been up to this time?' Lesley was smiling as she came into my study.

I hesitated. I knew she was pulling my leg, but still she was asking the question. And I could see that she was hiding something.

'Whatever it is, I deny all knowledge of it!' I smiled back at her.

'You naughty, naughty boy!' She pulled her hand out from behind her back and flourished a brown envelope at me. 'The bishop will throw the book at you if this ever gets out!'

'Why? What's in it? Let me have a look.'

'I don't know what's in it! It's what's on the outside that's so interesting.' She backed away from me, holding the envelope high.

I grabbed her round the waist and play-wrestled her to the floor. There, in huge red letters on the front of the envelope, were the words 'HM Customs Seizure Department'.

Lesley watched me, laughing at my horrified expression.

I'd ordered a video from a cult magazine in America. The UK customs had seized it, saying they considered it to be obscene material. I could not believe it. I'd always been a fan of Betty Page, one of the early American pin-ups of the 1950s. The film footage in question was mild compared to many films on general release but, as the letter explained, anything which included tying up was considered obscene. The more I explained it to Lesley, the funnier she seemed to find it, but I was convinced that, yet again, my career in the church was in jeopardy.

'Mark, I do love you.' She put her arms round me as I sat holding the letter and wondering what to do. 'You don't half get yourself into some awkward situations though.'

She was so right. Most of my mistakes were due to my own naivety and immaturity. My mental age was slow to catch up with my physical age. Sometimes I could be as innocent as a child – in stark contrast to my mature Anglican colleagues. Often, I despaired of myself. In my heart of hearts I still didn't feel that I was worthy to be a priest.

I felt so torn. I believed I had a message to proclaim and I wanted to bring people to faith, but I also knew that I couldn't hide the person I was. For one thing, everyone would see right through me! I knew that God loved me, warts and all. But being myself sometimes made other people in the church feel uncomfortable and unsettled. Being a priest isn't an easy job. All I could do was try my best to love my parishoners while helping them to discover the joy of walking by faith. I never felt I had all the answers, but I could share people's journeys, their trials and challenges, joys and sadness. The only thing I had to offer was the certainty that through the scriptures and the Holy Spirit we can know God intimately. And by believing him and acting on his word we can have a relationship with him that takes us beyond mere religion and church tradition.

I was so grateful that I'd married Lesley. She was so supportive and so non-judgmental. As she and I became more comfortable with our sexuality over the years it was not unusual for us to buy items from adult retailers. Our wedding night had been a disaster: we were both virgins and very naïve. We did know what to do, we just had problems doing it. It took two days to consummate our marriage. That was my fault, I'm afraid. Although, if Lesley had not insisted on wearing such tight jeans, things might have gone more smoothly! Since then we've grown together and become comfortable with being open about sex. We still have a lot to learn, and there are conflicts along the way, but we've found that it's better to address areas of difficulty openly and honestly rather than avoiding them or dismissing them as unimportant. I have seen so many marriages break up because the couples concerned are not open and honest about sex. It works both ways: men may be tempted to find sexual fulfilment outside marriage if their needs are not being met by their wife, but women can also feel trapped in a relationship where they are treated as sex objects, without love or respect, by their husbands.

I felt it was a pity that the church was not generally more open about sexuality. Although I'd only been a curate for a short time, I'd already had couples ask me for advice on sexual practices. I lent one couple a book I already had, warning them that they might need to be open-minded about some of the photographs and written material it contained. They found it refreshing and helpful and reading it breathed new life into their relationship, they told me.

I wrote back to HM Customs straight away, saying that I'd ordered the video in good faith, believing that the material was not offensive or obscene. I did not want to contest the seizure and asked them to destroy the tape. Interestingly enough, I later learnt that Betty Page herself had become a Christian and turned her back on the industry.

*

For a long time I'd been agonising over a very personal problem, which was causing me a lot of anxiety and depression. I'd consulted a specialist, and various doctors and lay people. Everyone said I should come out and not try to hide it, but I was too much of a coward. I was worried about how Lesley would react, and what people would think. How would Jonathan and Fiona feel about me? It was a big decision and I couldn't ignore it much longer.

I had first noticed the problem when I saw the back of my head in a mirror. I was horrified to discover that my crowning glory was thinning so much that I could see skin peeping through on the top of my head. I used every lotion and thickening shampoo on the market in a vain attempt to hold back the tide, but to no avail. It was getting worse. One GP suggested castration if I was that desperate. I was not amused, but I did manage to persuade him to prescribe a hair restoring product. I sent Lesley to the chemist to pick it up – along with our condoms – because I was too embarrassed to go myself.

'Shave it off,' said my old friend, Davo.

'Accept it,' advised my vicar Ian Davies. 'Just don't try and disguise it with a comb-over!'

The problem was, I could not accept it. I'd always had a mass of lovely hair, but now I was starting to look like Bruce Willis. And, to 'cap' it all, Jonathan and Fiona had started calling me 'baldy'!

Finally, when I was visiting Davo in Preston one day, he took me along to his hairdresser. I kept my eyes shut throughout the whole process. When I opened them, I looked like a cue ball.

'You look like a skinhead vicar,' laughed Lesley when I got home. 'Very menacing!'

I was so annoyed I locked myself in my study for the rest of the evening and was depressed for days. Jonathan and Fiona didn't help, they teased me mercilessly. Children can be cruel sometimes.

Then I decided to go public. I had good contacts at the local paper – in fact my nickname was Mr Fish-and-Chips as I was in the paper so much – and I suggested they ran a story on male baldness, using me as an example. Sure enough, within days the Northwest Evening Mail ran the story, 'Facing up to the bald facts', with the headline, 'Vicar prayed in vain for a cure.' Within weeks I'd recovered from the psychological trauma and got used to my new look. If anything, I wished I'd come out sooner. The new, slightly edgier, look gave me more street credibility with the youngsters on the estate. And I looked even more like Ian Davis's son. It didn't improve my squash game, though!

*

Life inside the curate's house in Barrow Island continued apace. The children were growing up and becoming young teenagers. When Lesley told me that Fiona had started her periods and bought a bra I nearly had a breakdown on the spot. I didn't cope well with change of any sort and I certainly didn't want my little girl to grow up. I covered my ears and started humming when Lesley tried to talk to me about it. It was painful for me to see Fiona's dolls being replaced by make-up and fashionable clothes. Jonathan's voice changed and his feet grew so much I thought he must be related to a Yeti. He'd soon be taller than me.

Lesley, as ever, took it all in her stride. But I had no idea how to be a parent to two teenagers. Jonathan in particular was becoming stroppy and sullen and inclined to challenge my authority. I felt frustrated and scared by his behaviour and often lost my temper. Lesley said she felt like the peacemaker between three warring factions in our house. That did not help – it just fuelled my own sense of insecurity. I was also starting to resent the fact that Lesley was always the good cop and I was always the bad one.

To be honest, all the confrontations and my wacky, excitable behaviour were a result of my internal struggle to control my own demons. I felt – and behaved – like a tiger on speed.

Professionally, I continued to function as a vicar. I did what was expected of me, but I was hiding behind the role. Deep down, I felt alienated from my family – and alienated from God. In the short term that wasn't a problem. I could gloss over it. Lesley and I were still very much in love, and it showed. I could still clown around with the kids and we had some great family times together. We did have fun, and both kids would still put their arms around me and say that they loved me.

There were long periods when everything seemed fine, then something would act as a trigger and I would lose it. I always ended up sitting on the floor, crying, with Lesley hugging and comforting me. I hated myself and I hated losing control, but I seemed unable to break the cycle of behaviour that had been going on for years now.

The only person I could confide in was Gerald, the spiritual director I'd met while I was in hospital. I knew he believed in sacramental confession and whatever I said to him would never be disclosed to anyone else. But I'd grown up trusting no one and I'd been let down so many times that I still found it hard to be truly open with people. I felt so guilty before God that I could hardly lift my head to him in prayer. Here I was, a priest, but slowly dying on the inside. I couldn't even tell Lesley how bad I felt.

My answer to my spiritual crisis was to become more religious. I used the prayer book liturgy more and more in my own daily devotions. I used more formal, written-down prayers. I hung crucifixes on the wall to help me focus more on Christ and his suffering. I crossed myself more frequently and made a big thing of celebrating Mass. I knew I was overcompensating but I felt I needed to do it, in order to maintain my integrity as a priest. I did not want to destroy the image I believed people had of a priest as someone who spends all day doing holy things.

As a vicar it's very easy to find yourself living a lie, not intentionally deceiving people, but needing to play the role of the perfect priest for the sake of others. Fortunately, not everyone is like that. I'm so grateful for the many people I have met down the years who have allowed me to be myself. I thank God for their love and friendship. It is they who have kept me sane during the most difficult and challenging times in my life.

As my curacy entered its fourth year I found myself on a religious treadmill. It was better than nothing. And maybe if I struggled on, I would eventually rediscover the intimacy with God I once knew. For now, though, I was clinging to that old rugged cross as if my life depended on it.

*

The summer of 1999 was a particularly hot one. After our usual break down south we made the most of the time before Jonathan and Fiona had to go back to school by going out as a family whenever Lesley and I weren't working. Living in Barrow we could be sitting beside the lake eating ice cream, or by the sea at Morecombe, in under an hour. Even parish life seemed to slow down, apart from the occasional wedding or funeral.

August 12 was a memorable day for two reasons. It was Fiona's birthday, always a big event in our household. This year she was given the first of what was to be a string of mobile phones – a marriage for life, I called it!

It was also the day that Ian Davies invited me out for lunch and dropped a bombshell. I was suspicious from the moment I took the call from him.

'Why is he asking me out to lunch?' I said to Lesley. 'He never takes me out to lunch. We normally have lunch at the vicarage.'

'Don't be so paranoid, Mark.' Lesley patted my hand reassuringly. 'He probably just wants to catch up with you after the holidays. First we were away, then he was, so you haven't seen each other for a while.'

'No, something's going on.' I felt nervy and irritated. 'He wouldn't ask me out unless he was up to something.'

'Well, you'd better get yourself along to the Owl and Pussycat and find out what, then, hadn't you!'

I arrived at 12.30. I knew why Ian had chosen the Owl and Pussycat – their two-for-one lunch deal. I couldn't argue with that! Ian arrived ten minutes later, looking his usual bouncy self.

'Hiya Mark! Had a good holiday?' he said cheerily.

'Yeah, not bad thanks.' I tried to smile but I was feeling churned up inside. I noticed that Ian had his briefcase with him. Why on earth had he brought his briefcase to lunch?

We made small talk as we waited for our meals to arrive. Despite my paranoia, I was hungry and my 14oz steak was a welcome sight. I was just about to put the first juicy chunk into my mouth when Ian spoke.

'Now, Mark, the real reason I asked you to lunch is that the bishop wants you to consider moving to your own parish. St Francis is only the other side of town.'

I went completely off my steak and just sat there in suspended animation, the fork hovering in the air.

'So what do you think?' Ian asked. He smiled at me encouragingly.

'Think? I think I'm going to be sick!' Slowly I put the fork back down on my plate. I'd lost my appetite. 'It's a bit of a shock. I thought I had another year to go on my licence.'

'Yes, that's right,' Ian confirmed. 'But the truth is, you've outgrown your ministry on Barrow Island. You've proved everyone wrong and become a fine priest and the best pastor I've ever known. You've been an inspiration to my own ministry. I can only wish I had the pastoral gifts that you have.'

I didn't know what to say. Hearing Ian compliment me like that was very moving. But I did not feel ready to go solo. I picked at my food and left the restaurant in a solemn mood.

'How did it go?' asked Lesley brightly as I walked through the door.

'The bishop wants me to consider moving to St Francis as my first posting,' I announced.

'That's wonderful!' Lesley jumped up and down and was very excited about the prospect. Just the reaction I didn't want or need. I retreated to my study and curled up on the settee in the foetal position. I was depressed for days.

I was scared to death of another move. I didn't feel nearly as ready to take on my own church as the bishop and Ian thought I was, and I couldn't imagine how I'd cope. I was even beginning to wish I hadn't done such a good job on Barrow Island.

All my insecurities came rushing to the surface with a vengeance. The experiences of my childhood, which included having four different foster homes between the ages of three and nine, still cast a long shadow over my present. Although on one level I'd got used to being moved from pillar to post, as an adult I hated the thought of being uprooted, even if it was just across town. My biggest consolation was that Ian Davis would still be around to mentor and encourage me.

Lesley, with her normal wisdom, understood why I was reacting the way I was. She did her best to reassure me that it wouldn't be so bad once we were settled in. My lovely wife, she was used to these times of regression when she had to be parent to three children, not two. Her unconditional love for me never wavered, she never thought badly of me and was always there to put her arms round me and comfort me. It was during those times that I was most aware of God's very real presence in Lesley. Only someone full of the love of God would be able to put up with my mood swings and my temper tantrums.

How I envied her sense of security and peace. She wasn't daunted by the prospect of another move. Neither were Jonathan or Fiona. They would just have a slightly longer walk to school.

Over the next few weeks, I gradually began to adjust to the idea. I was inevitably going to have to go somewhere as my curacy drew to an end, and it was better to stay in Barrow than move away completely. In the meantime, I was sworn to secrecy until everything was finalised between St John's and the two churches I would be going to, St Matthew's and St Francis'.

'I don't have a clue how to run a parish,' I confessed to Ian over coffee one day.

'That's OK, neither does the rector you'll be working for!' he joked.

My new rector was to be David Kennedy, a small Irish man who had been a school teacher and college chaplain before becoming a vicar. He had only been licensed to St Matthews in 1999. I'd been at that service myself, little thinking that so soon I'd be working with him as team vicar of St Francis with St Matthews.

CHAPTER FOUR

My licensing and induction service took place on 30 March 2000. As a vicar, my term of office would be for seven years, extendable at the bishop's discretion. The green pews of St Francis' church, a red-brick building with plain windows and a wooden floor, were packed with well-wishers and supporters from St John's and colleagues from other churches in the town. Bishop Ian Harland delivered a very personal address and there were sniggers and winks from some of my closest friends when he spoke about Lesley whipping me into shape and keeping me grounded!

'What have you been saying to the bishop, you bad boy?' Lesley whispered, poking me in the ribs.

'Nothing,' I protested, trying to look innocent.

When the time came for me to swear allegiance to God, the Queen and the Church, I did so with gusto. I was relieved that, once the service was over, the real work could begin.

I knew it wouldn't be easy, but I was determined to establish myself at the heart of the community. The Ormsgill estate had the reputation of being one of the most deprived areas in the whole of Cumbria. The people there wouldn't take kindly to any sort of authority figure and I knew I'd have to prove myself before they would accept me.

Where should I begin?

The best place to start, I was sure, was outside the confines of the church building. I needed to get out and simply walk the streets of my new parish. So, on my first day as vicar – rather nervously - that's exactly what I did.

I was pleasantly surprised to discover that the area wasn't as bad as I'd been led to believe. Yes, there were some obvious signs of deprivation, but nothing a lick of paint or a trip to the local tip would not solve. Not everyone was pleased to see their new priest walking around the estate, however, and they were not backward in making their feelings known. Some people ignored me completely while others slammed the door in my face when I knocked. The local youths let rip with the usual stream of profanities. I did not let it get to me. In fact, I felt completely at home there. I'd been brought up on a very similar estate and felt that these were my kind of people. And my whole reason for being there was to share the love of God and show the people that his love wasn't contained inside the church building.

The first place I called, on that first day, was the post office. Wearing my leather jacket and baseball cap, the staff eyed me with suspicion at first. I looked as though I was casing the joint, until I turned round and they saw my dog collar. Peter and Linda, the sub postmaster and postmistress, were to become extremely supportive of my ministry. Peter was a very hardworking business man, who didn't suffer fools gladly. A staunch Catholic, his wisdom was always spot on, as I discovered when I sat on various community committees and school governing bodies with him. I knew I could always count on Peter when I needed to discuss issues surrounding the estate or the church or the school. I loved spending time in the post office over the years. It was where I met most of my flock. Not the church-goers so much, but those on the fringe, the people who felt excluded from traditional religion and out of place in church. They were happy to approach me in the post office to ask me to pray for them, or inquire about baptisms, weddings, and funerals. Everyone soon got used to seeing the priest in the leather jacket and baseball cap loitering with intent somewhere between the sweets and the deli counter.

During my time serving the community of Ormsgill I discovered that almost anything might be required of me. There were the normal pastoral concerns, focusing on births, deaths and marriages. Although, as people living together was the norm, I actually took relatively few marriages while I was on the estate.

I found myself trying to help and support my flock in a whole variety of situations and difficulties. These included mental illness, terminal illness, miscarriage, stillbirth, divorce, abuse, drug addiction, alcoholism, suicide, child protection issues, feuds, debt and evictions. I was privileged to stand alongside people, sharing their good times and walking with them in dark times.

I loved every minute of my ministry in Ormsgill. Despite its reputation for drugs, anti-social behaviour and crime, I found the majority of the people there to be warm, friendly and hospitable.

*

During my first week as vicar of St Francis', I was coming out of church after taking the mid-week service when I saw a young woman running towards me. She looked agitated.

'Vicar,' she shouted. 'Can you help me?'

'Yes, of course, if I can. What's the problem?'

'It's not me, vicar, it's my friend Kerry. Her house is haunted and she's freaking out.'

'Oh, great,' I thought. 'Just what I need. A hysterical woman thinking she's seen a ghost.'

'OK, not a problem,' I said out loud, trying to sound reassuring. 'Where does Kerry live?'

'Over there,' said the young woman, pointing in the direction of the as yet unoccupied vicarage. 'Come with me and I'll take you to her,' she continued urgently. 'She's in a right state.'

I locked the church and followed her across the road to the housing association estate which had been built on land formerly owned by the church, right at the back of the vicarage. St Francis Gardens was a mixture of two bedroom houses and one bedroom flats. The young woman let us into one of the houses.

'Kerry, it's Kim. I've brought the vicar to see you.'

The first thing I noticed about Kerry was how beautiful she was. But, hunched up on the settee in the living room, with her knees held tight to her chest and her face partly hidden by her long, light brown hair, she was clearly very upset.

I sat down beside her.

'Hello Kerry, I'm Father Mark, the new vicar from St Francis. Would you like to tell me what's been happening?'

Kerry looked up at me with tear-stained eyes.

'I'm sorry Father Mark, you must think I'm barmy.'

'No, of course not,' I felt a little overawed by her beauty, but I knew I must remain professional and find out what was going on.

Kerry explained that her partner had just walked out, leaving her and her three-year-old daughter, Holly. Holly's father had abandoned Kerry on Christmas Eve three years before, when Kerry was about to give birth. This new break-up had left Kerry alone and distressed again – and strange things had started happening in the house. Doors banged for no apparent reason and footsteps sounded on the stairs.

'I'm sorry, Father Mark, you must think I'm some sort of neurotic woman.' Kerry straightened up and tried to compose herself.

I tried to look unflappable but inwardly I was wondering what to do next.

'Kerry, please don't be offended, but I feel I should ask you – have you been smoking anything that could be causing hallucinations?'

She laughed a little. 'No, of course not. I used to, but not anymore.'

'Well, tell me more about what happened today then.'

Upset by the recent break-up, Kerry had gone to lie down for a while. Holly was being looked after by Kerry's aunt to give Kerry some time to herself. But no sooner had Kerry closed her eyes than the wardrobe door had started banging and she felt a wind blowing over her. The windows were all tight shut and she freaked out.

Part of me thought that this sort of manifestation isn't uncommon when someone has been through a dramatic and difficult event. I don't understand the science behind it, but I do know that strong emotions can cause brain waves to trigger all kinds of disturbances.

I sat there for what seemed like ages. I must admit, I was captivated by Kerry. Eventually it occurred to me that if I was there much longer, all sorts of rumours might start flying around.

'Why don't I come back tomorrow?' I suggested, getting up. 'I'll bring some holy water to sprinkle, and say some prayers. How does that sound?'

Kerry seemed delighted by this idea and by the time I left she was smiling. She also promised to come to church the following Sunday.

After my visit the next day, the disturbances stopped and Kerry said the house felt different. And, true to her word, Kerry and Holly came along to church. I introduced them to Lesley after the service and they chatted for ages.

Kerry became very good friends with us as a family while I was at St Francis. She and I were alike in many ways and we developed a special friendship. I know it's unwise for a married man to get close to another woman, and clergy guidelines positively discourage friendship with the opposite sex. But my relationship with Kerry included Lesley and the rest of the family, it was never secretive – and Lesley, bless her, approved and trusted us both.

Kerry helped keep me grounded and never let me forget that I was first and foremost a human being, and a priest second. She attended St Francis for a while, but I felt that she needed to be in a church with more people her own age – she was only 27 and the congregation of St Francis was quite elderly. I eventually put her in touch with another church which had a lot more going on for her and Holly. Our loss was their gain. She settled well at Spring Mount Christian Fellowship and made many friends.

*

As I settled into life at St Francis, it was great to have the congregation supporting me in what I did best – bringing new people into the church from the Ormsgill estate. Wherever I went in the parish, children and young people would talk to me and shout, 'Hiya, Father Mark!' from across the street. I was beginning to feel accepted. More families started to attend morning worship and the services inevitably got noisier. Special services like Christmas and Easter, and a new All Souls service which I combined with St Francis Tide, drew particularly large congregations, which most people thought was a wonderful development.

Not everyone was pleased with the changes, however. Matters came to a head over the tricky issue of vestments.

I was now a governor of the school on the estate, and the schoolchildren began coming to visit the church with their teachers as part of their religious education. They wanted to know more about Christianity and the Church of England. Wanting to make their visits fun as well as educational, I let them dress up in all the vestments, which they loved. But for some members of the congregation, this was sacrilege, and, combined with the noisy services, meant that some people felt unable to continue attending.

What could I do? I was sorry that people were unhappy, but how could I object to new people coming to church and children having a good time?

I was still struggling with my own faith. On the outside, I was doing everything a parish priest should do – taking services, conducting weddings and funerals, christening children, caring and praying for people in need. I'd cleared out the rubbish from behind the church building and smartened up the interior. Unfortunately the physical clear-out hadn't been matched by a spiritual one inside me. I'd lost my own intimacy with God and my sense of his presence. So I clung more and more to tradition and ritual. Since coming to St Francis, I'd introduced the Stations of the Cross, a reserved sacrament light in the sanctuary, the ringing of the bell during Mass and the swinging of incense at high services. I liked to be called 'Father Mark.'

I shared my feelings with my rector, David Kennedy, a lovely, spirit-filled man and a great pastor. Under his ministry St Matthews, St Francis' mother church, grew considerably, but David was having problems with some members of his congregation, just as I was with some of mine. His biggest battle came over the timing of the morning service, which he wanted to change to a later time and make more suitable for the young families who were starting to attend church. I couldn't have wished for a better colleague than David – humble, self-effacing and extremely supportive of my own ministry.

*

'Come home quick,' read the text message. 'I'm ovulating!' Not the sort of thing you expect to hear from your wife while you're conducting a funeral service.

'Oh joy,' I thought. 'Here we go again.'

Lesley and I had been trying for another baby for a couple of years. Jonathan and Fiona were growing up and we were getting broody. Every time I held a child at a baptismal service I thought how lovely it would be to have a baby in the house again. But Lesley was 40 and I was 39 and things just didn't seem to be happening.

We sought medical advice.

I arrived at the fertility clinic just after taking the midweek service, wearing my black suit and clerical collar, and was slightly taken aback when the young nurse handed me a specimen bottle.

'I'm really sorry, but I've just been to the toilet. I think it might be difficult to produce a specimen,' I whispered.

'Father,' she smiled, 'That's not the sort of specimen we need you to provide.'

'What? You've got to be kidding!'

'Sorry, but this is a fertility clinic. We've got to cover all the bases…'

She showed me into a room and asked if I needed any men's magazines. I just wanted the floor to open and swallow me up. How I wished I hadn't worn my dog collar.

When I got home from my appointment, Kerry was having coffee with Lesley. They both went into hysterics as I told them what had happened, and demanded to know which magazine I'd opted for. I tried to see the funny side but I was too embarrassed and rather cross with them.

As soon as the funeral was over, I got home as quickly as I could, knowing that Lesley would be waiting. She jumped on me the minute I got through the door. My dog collar and clothes were littered all over the stairs as she undressed me on the way to the bedroom. I nearly fell backwards in my haste to remove my socks. Her skimpy outfit left nothing to the imagination and it was certainly having the desired effect on me.

Although, by now the routine was all too familiar. We made love several times whenever Lesley was ovulating, but it was becoming increasingly mechanical. Lesley became inventive in dressing up to excite me, but despite us both doing our best to maintain a mixture of spice and romance in the bedroom, each time she failed to conceive we became more despondent. It was heartbreaking every time she told me, sobbing, that her period had started.

We did all we could to improve our chances. Apparently the fault was largely mine – I didn't have enough swimmers to do the job. So I avoided hot baths and started wearing loose boxer shorts. Every time we made love, Lesley had to lie still, with her lower body raised, to give what swimmers I did produce as much help as possible. The hospital wasn't offering IVF and in any case there was no way we could afford it on a vicar's stipend.

After nearly three years of trying, even we had to agree with the hospital's conclusion that it was very unlikely we'd ever have any more children. It was crushing to be told the news by the consultant. We just held each other and sobbed.

'What are we going to do now, Mark?' Lesley asked, tears streaming down her face. 'It's too late. We're past it.'

'I don't know, love.' I hugged her tight. 'We should pray about it, I suppose. After all, God can do anything, can't he?' I tried to sound spiritual and reassuring, but I didn't even convince myself. Not really.

For the next few months David, the rector, came round once a week to lay hands on me and Lesley and pray for us to conceive. Even our new bishop, Bishop Graham, prayed for us when we met him for the first time. I was sorry when Bishop Ian had retired: he'd taken a chance on me and I'd always appreciated his concern for me and my family when my first curacy hadn't worked out.

My first meeting with Bishop Graham didn't start too well.

'We do serve a wonderful God, don't we Mark?' The bishop shook my hand, a cheerful smile spreading across his face. 'We're so blessed!'

Not the way I was feeling, I wasn't. I couldn't stop myself blurting out that everything in my garden was far from rosy.

When the bishop offered to pray for us I was reluctant at first, but what had we got to lose? If I'm honest, I was jealous of his certainty and closeness to God. I longed for that kind of relationship myself, but my heart was cold and I was still battling with depression and insecurity. I was hiding my crisis of faith behind a professional exterior. But my family could see I was on a downward spiral, and our struggles to have another baby were making my feelings of isolation and despair even more acute.

I still believed in a big God, however. A God who answers prayer. One day in late November I was getting more and more upset as I was praying about our desire to have more children. I've never been much of a one for having special 'words' from God, but this time I thought I felt God say to me, 'Lesley will conceive.' I wrote the words in my Bible. I was reluctant to tell Lesley, and to risk getting her hopes up again, but as soon as I shared with her what I felt God had said, she believed it. I did so hope that I was right. But as the days went on, I began to doubt. Had it really been God speaking, or was it just my wishful thinking? Although I tried to be faithful to what I believed was a promise from God, doubt and fear crept back in. I tried to hide my growing disillusionment from everyone except Lesley and David, the rector. He continued to come and pray for us regularly.

*

I will never forget the sunny day the following July when I was working in my study and heard a sudden cry from upstairs. I dashed out of the room and saw Lesley standing on the landing, crying hysterically.

'What's the matter? What is it, love?'

She couldn't speak, but, with tears pouring down her face, she held out her hand to me. I could see something plastic. I rushed up the stairs - I thought she was trying to give me a toothbrush.

'What's that?'

'I'm pregnant!' she cried, thrusting the test kit into my hands.

'Are you sure?' I could hardly believe what she was saying.

'Look at the indicator. It's changed colour!'

Sure enough, it had.

I grabbed hold of Lesley and hugged her. We both stood there, arms round each other, weeping with joy.

Eventually Lesley pulled away. 'We still need to have it confirmed by the doctor,' she said.

'I know. But – I've got to tell someone!' I couldn't contain my excitement.

I knew just who to ring. My friend Davo and I had spoken twice a week on the phone ever since our time as students together. Whereas by nature I'm open and upfront about things, Davo is completely the opposite – secretive even. A good person to confide in.

In my excitement, I dialled a wrong number twice. At last Davo answered.

'Davo, it's me. Guess what? Lesley's pregnant!'

He was delighted for us, but, cautious as ever, advised not getting too carried away until we'd had the news confirmed.

'You've been disappointed before, Mark, you know.'

He was right, of course. But this time it was different. Our prayers had been answered. My wife really was expecting a baby.

I swear I went round for weeks with a permanent grin on my face, thinking I was a super stud. OK, it had taken a long time, but even my slow swimmers had got there in the end. It was a relief all round: no more boxer shorts, no more text messages summoning me home at inappropriate moments, no more flow charts, no more rather clinical sex.

Gradually, as the news sunk in, we began to tell people. The congregation at St Francis was delighted, as was the rector, who had faithfully continued to pray for us all that time. Jonathan and

Fiona were both thrilled at the prospect of having a baby brother or sister.

*

While we were on our annual summer holiday down south, we decided to break the good news to Lesley's parents. We hadn't told them we were trying for a baby – as far as they were concerned, we were looking forward to packing Jonathan and Fiona off to university before too long.

Lesley was in the phone box for ages. I kept banging on the glass, anxious to know what her mother was saying, but Lesley just shook her fist at me and turned away, laughing.

Eventually she emerged.

'Well? What did she say?' I asked.

'She's pleased for us.' Lesley said demurely.

'Is that all? It took you long enough to find that out!'

'Oh, you know, there was all the usual stuff, like, have I had a scan, and aren't I a bit old for a new baby, and how are we going to afford it?'

'Hmm, yes, fair enough. I guess they just want to be sure we're being sensible.'

'Let's hope it's not twins, then,' joked Lesley. 'Otherwise we really will be in the poor house.'

Later that evening, Lesley was admiring her bump in the mirror.

'Mark, do you think I'm a bit big for 10 weeks?'

I looked at her bump and wondered, how big are you meant to be anyway?

'Nah, you look fine,' I said casually.

For the rest of the holiday Lesley felt sick and kept having to rush off to the loo. She avoided doing anything too strenuous, but kept to the shade and watched from the pier as Jonathan and I swam in the sea and Fiona sunbathed. I thought Lesley was getting a bit obsessed by her size, but I made light of it.

Back in Barrow I was quickly thrown back into parish life. We'd calculated that the baby was due in March 2002. My sister Shene hoped it would be born on March 18th, her birthday – and her twin's.

I was in my study one day, working on a sermon, when the door opened and my friend Davo from Preston wandered in.

'Hey, Mark.'

'Hey yourself!'

'Where's Lesley? I'm hungry.'

'At the hospital having a scan. She's been gone ages. What do you think? Shall we go and get fish and chips?'

I was interrupted by the phone ringing.

'It's me,' said Lesley, unnecessarily. 'I've had the scan.'

'Great! Is it a boy or a girl?'

There was a short silence. I felt unnerved. Was something wrong?

'Mark? Are you sitting down?'

'Why? What's the matter?' I could feel panic starting to rise inside me.

'I'm expecting twins!'

I was so stunned I could not speak. Davo relieved me of the phone, which was dangling from my hand, and listened to Lesley for a minute or two.

'My word. My word,' he said. 'Twins! My word.'

When Lesley got home she showed us the picture and, sure enough, you could just make out two little shapes.

'How do you feel, Lesley?' I wanted to know.

'It's a bit scary, but wonderful! After three years of trying, all those tests, then being told we'd never have any more children, it's a real blessing from God to be expecting two at once!'

Davo and I went off to get the fish and chips.

'Yes love, what can I get you?' asked the woman behind the counter.

'Twins, please,' I said, my mind on other things.

'Eh?'

Davo stepped in. 'You'd best ignore him, you won't get any sense out of him today,' he said, and took over, placing our order.

Lesley spent ages on the phone that evening, telling all our friends and family the news. My sister Shene was particularly delighted. During the Sunday morning service I announced that we were expecting twins and the whole church erupted with a spontaneous round of applause.

*

As the weeks passed, Lesley grew bigger and bigger. She was so uncomfortable in bed that she often went to sleep in the spare room. Trips to the baby shop became a weekly event, but mostly we were just window shopping. Now that we were buying for two it was a real blessing that we found a good second hand buggy. Kerry gave us Holly's old cot and we bought a second one from an advertisement in the paper. Lesley planned to take full maternity leave from her job with Cumbria Care but we couldn't afford her to stop working altogether, we needed the second income.

We knew that making ends meet would be a challenge, but we also believed that we could depend on God to meet our daily needs. Throughout our married life we'd always taken seriously the biblical principle of tithing – that is, giving away ten per cent of our income. It was part of our discipline as followers of Jesus. Over the years, we'd given over and above the ten per cent, and we'd seen God bless us, financially and in other ways. So, despite the fact that we felt it was sensible to stick to a budget, we firmly believed that God would provide for us. And he did.

It was Lesley who was in charge of the money in our house. She was really good at it and always knew, to the penny, what was coming in and what was going out. We believed it was our Christian responsibility not to get into debt, to pay our bills on time, and not to buy things we couldn't afford. The only trouble was, I felt less of a man because I was hopeless with finance. But Lesley, bless her, knew how to handle me sensitively, and would just tell me it was 'that time' again, when I had to sign things or go to the bank.

Soon, two Moses baskets sat on their stands in the spare bedroom. The double pram was in the hall, near the front door. The drawers were filling up with nappies and other baby stuff. It was all rather exciting.

Exciting – but scary. Would we be able to afford to look after four children? How would we cope when Lesley went back to work? Neither of us was getting any younger – how would we cope with two screaming babies night after night?

I tried to imagine holding two babies at the same time and practised in the spare bedroom, cooing to my non-existent infants. Lesley caught me at it and gave me a huge hug. It was then that we felt one of the babies kick for the first time. We both cried with joy.

CHAPTER FIVE

I was exhausted when I arrived home after taking two funerals and the midweek healing service at St Francis. One of the funerals in particular had been emotionally draining. A young girl had tragically taken her own life. I'd sat with the family over the preceding days, walking with them in their grief, but how could I find words to comfort them? My own life had nearly ended at 18, but my suicide attempt had been more of a cry for help than a real desire to end it all, and it had failed.

I walked into the kitchen to see Lesley standing with her back to the sink, a worried expression on her face. After 15 years of marriage it was easy to tell that something was wrong.

'What's up, love?'

'Sweetheart, it's your dad.'

'My dad? What about him?'

I hadn't seen my dad for years, and the last time we met he'd completely blanked me, making a fuss of Lesley and the kids instead. That was hurtful, but Lesley explained it was probably because he didn't know how to relate to me, as he'd spent very little time with me while I was growing up. We certainly didn't have much of a relationship, Dad and me.

'Your sister Shene called. Your dad's in hospital and they think he's dying. Shene and Graham are heading over to Boston to see him this afternoon. She said not to go rushing over because she knows you have your hands full here.'

Lesley followed me as I walked into my study.

'Mark? Are you OK?'

I sighed, then nodded. 'Yes, I think so. I'm just not sure what I'm meant to feel, that's all.'

Lesley sat on my knee and tenderly stroked my balding head. I was sad to hear that my dad was so ill. But I was a priest – I often sat with dying people, gave them the last rites, and took funerals. It was part of my job to minister to the sick and prepare the dying for death. I always felt sad and compassionate towards the ill and the bereaved. Some deaths had more of an effect on me than others. The death of a close friend from my congregation, or the death of a baby or child was always very upsetting. Now it was my own dad who was dying, and I felt guilty that the news didn't seem to mean anything in particular to me.

But I was in pain - although it had nothing to do with my dad...

'Lesley!'

'What, honey?'

'You're a heavy lump and you're sitting on my groin. Get off!'

I eased her off my knee.

'Shall I rub it better?' she asked, grinning.

'No thanks, you've done enough damage already! My goodness, you are a weight.'

'Watch it! Just remember they're your twins!'

Dad was in hospital for two weeks. He'd been in and out of hospital many times before and recovered, and I think we all assumed it'd be the same this time. So everyone was surprised when he died. My sisters Shene, Maxine and Jenny started to make the funeral arrangements.

*

'Fram?' It was six years since I'd seen my childhood friend, but now I needed a favour from him. It was good to hear his voice on the phone.

'Teddy Edwards! Long time no speak! What can I do for you?'

'It's my dad, Fram. He's just died, and the funeral's going to be in Boston. Any chance of us coming to stay with you, buddy?'

Fram was sad to hear about my dad, but delighted at the prospect of seeing us all again. The arrangements began falling into place: I was to do a gospel reading at the service and I planned to wear my clerical robes for the occasion. I was pleased that representatives from the Burma Star Association would be in attendance and would lower the standard at the appropriate time. I knew that Dad, an ex-soldier who had served in the Burma campaign, would like that.

The congregation at St Francis were all lovely when I announced during the Sunday service that I'd be away next week, burying my dad. I knew it would be a tough week and I'd need plenty of prayer support. Tensions and emotions in my family were running high. I was expecting my brother Paul to come to the funeral. He was still struggling with the legacy of our childhood and, despite his faith, was emotionally vulnerable. Part of the problem was that he'd joined the Navy soon after leaving the children's home and had become thoroughly institutionalised. After leaving the Navy he was diagnosed with a depressive anxiety disorder and hadn't really worked since, although he was very willing and would do anything to help anybody.

After church, Kerry and Holly were due to come to lunch with us. Holly came storming in, her usual hyperactive self, and started trying to climb all over Jonathan, who at 16 was not amused.

'Holly! If you don't behave, you know what will happen,' Kerry warned.

At only four, Holly was very cute and very opinionated. She tossed her head, turned on her heels and disappeared upstairs with Fiona. She knew that if she pushed her mum too far she'd get a smacked bottom. Kerry was a perfect mum: strict but loving, she knew that Holly needed a firm hand. Kerry helped Lesley with the lunch while I pottered in the study. After lunch I told Lesley to go and put her feet up while Kerry and I did the dishes. Holly sat at the table with her colouring book.

'How are you doing since your dad died, Mark?' Kerry asked, coming straight to the point as usual.

'Oh, fine thanks.' I didn't want to talk about it. She gave me a stern look, but let it go.

When we'd finished the dishes, Kerry took a cup of tea in to Lesley and I went and flopped into the chair in my study.

Minutes later, Kerry followed me with a cup of coffee in her hand.

'How was your church this morning?' I asked.

'Never mind church. Tell me, how are you really feeling about your dad?'

'Fine. Really.'

'Mark! I'm one of your closest friends. Please don't hide your feelings.' Her eyes were starting to flash, but I didn't want to be drawn into conversation.

'Kerry, I'm a priest. I'm used to dealing with death and bereavement. I'm meant to be in control. I can handle it.'

I knew immediately that I'd said the wrong thing. Her face was like thunder.

'I'm not having it, Mark. It's not fair on your friends or your family when you keep hiding your feelings behind that bloody dog collar. I've just been talking to Lesley and she's really worried about you.'

I had to admit she was right. But I didn't want to share my struggles with anyone, least of all Lesley, who was working so hard and was so tired with carrying the twins. Her hormones were in such a mess, she kept breaking down in tears. The last thing I wanted was to add to her burdens. But maybe it would be a relief to talk to someone.

'Sorry, Kerry. You're right, I am struggling. I've got lots of regrets. There are things I'd like to have said to Dad, and I'm sorry I wasn't there for him when he died. I didn't realise how ill he was, though - I thought Shene might have been exaggerating.' As I started to talk, I realised that my reactions weren't as straightforward as I'd first thought. 'I think the biggest thing is that I feel guilty. Guilty for not feeling anything.'

'Have you shared any of this with Lesley?'

'No – I didn't want to upset her. Things are tough enough for her at the moment.'

'Idiot. She needs you to be open with her, you should know that. You need to talk to her.'

'OK,' I muttered. 'No more hiding behind the dog collar.'

Kerry's smile returned. 'Good. I told Lesley I'd sort you out.' She gave me a friendly punch on the shoulder and left the study to drink her coffee with Lesley.

*

We finally arrived at Fram and Joel's house after five hours in the car. It was lovely to see Fram and Joel and their beautiful children. Fram had had a difficult time with leukaemia, but thankfully the disease was now in remission and he looked fit and well. Joel was as lovely as ever and fussed over Lesley like a mother hen.

Later that evening, I called my sister Jenny to find out what time we were to meet at the chapel of rest. I was staggered to hear that she hadn't had a visit from the vicar about the service, which was due to happen the next day.

'What, you're telling me you haven't spoken to him at all?'

'No, not since two days ago. I phoned him to ask when he would be coming to see me and he said today. It's nearly six o'clock and he still hasn't been. Mark, what should I do?' She sounded very anxious.

'Give me his number. I'll call him.'

I dialled the number she gave me and waited. I was beginning to think I'd just get an answering machine, when a very American-sounding voice said hello. I explained who I was, and said I'd be doing a reading at the service and that I was calling because my sister was expecting a visit from him which hadn't materialised. I was totally flummoxed by his response.

'I think God is saying that you should take your dad's funeral, Mark.'

I was speechless. He said it again:

'Mark, I really think that God is telling me you should take the service tomorrow.'

What could I say? I couldn't argue with God.

'Oh… fine. Leave it with me.'

I put the phone down and sat there in a daze. I'd just agreed to take my own dad's funeral and I knew almost nothing about him, except that he was in the army.

Lesley came in and saw me.

'Mark, whatever's the matter? You've gone white!'

'I'm doing the funeral tomorrow.'

'What? No you're not, that's ridiculous!'

'I am. The curate said God was telling him I should do it. So what could I say? I'm going to have to.'

'Oh Mark, that's so insensitive and unfair. What are you going to do?'

My brain was just starting to work again. 'I'll call Jenny and tell her what's happening, and get as much information from her about Dad as I can.'

I'd fill in the blanks in Dad's story by simply talking about how Dad was made in God's image and was loved by him, warts and all. I'd have to be honest about the fact that Dad hadn't be able to look after me and my brother Paul. I knew that he'd tried, but each time it went wrong and Paul and I ended up back in care. Dad did his best, within his own limitations, and I couldn't fault him for that. I could also speak about Dad's pride when I met and married Lesley – he called her a diamond. It would amuse people to hear that Dad thought Lesley was an artist when I told him she had a Bachelor of Arts degree. And the incident when he'd nearly set fire to Maxine was funny too. In the car on the way back from my wedding he threw his cigarette out of the front window, only for it to come straight back in through the open rear window and land on Maxine…

I finished writing up the service by about midnight. It had been a long day. Lesley had texted Kerry, who had told as many people as possible from St Francis that I was having to take my dad's funeral. They were all praying for me.

We set off in plenty of time from Fram's house the following morning. Fiona and Jonathan didn't want to come to the funeral, so Joel and Fram kindly offered to look after them until Lesley and I got back. By the time I was standing in the warm spring sunshine outside the chapel of rest, waiting for Shene and Graham to arrive, I was feeling very emotional and uptight. The only way I could handle things was by thinking of myself as Dad's priest, not his son.

Lesley and Graham didn't want to come and view the body, so Shene and I went in together and stood looking down at the open coffin. There was my dad, his full head of grey hair neatly combed, and dressed, as he always was, in a suit and tie. He always took pride in his appearance.

I bit my lip and swallowed. I mustn't cry, I must hold it together, I thought. I could do this. My religious role was the only protection I had against the pain twisting inside me. I could hear Shene sobbing, and I reached out and held her hand.

An image came powerfully into my mind as we stood there. My dad, taking me and Paul in the middle of the night, with our little suitcases, to Aunty Violet and Uncle Frank's house, after Dad had had a row with his landlady. Early the following morning we sat on the steps of Boston social services department, waiting for the offices to open. Once they had, Paul and I waited patiently on the hard seats in the corridor and watched Dad, behind the frosted glass panel, speaking to the social worker for what seemed like ages. At last, Dad emerged. He walked right past us and down the spiral staircase, without saying a word. Later that morning, as we were driven away to a new foster home, I looked back out of the rear window of the social worker's car and saw Dad leaning up against a shop window, smoking a cigarette and watching us. He looked smaller and smaller as we drove away.

Shene squeezed my hand and wiped away a tear. I took out my purple stole, kissed it and placed it around my neck. Taking out my prayer book, I turned to the last rites and prayer for absolution and commendation for the dear departed soul.

I did what I had to do.

By the time I finished, I could hardly see the words on the page because of the tears. I reached out to touch my father's hands, lying crossed in the centre of his body. I squeezed them and said the words I'd never had the chance to say while he was alive, 'I love you, Dad. I forgive you.'

Did I have regrets? Yes, of course I did. Maybe I could have done more to try and build a relationship with my dad. But he was a difficult man to get to know. He could be very abrasive and he never showed much emotion – except when his beloved football team, Boston United, scored a goal So long as he could live in his own little world, have the odd pint at his local, and meet his pals for a game of dominoes, he was happy. I didn't blame him for the way he was. He was a decent man, he just couldn't cope with all the family responsibilities he had, although he tried his best.

'Rest in peace, Dad,' I whispered. I took off the purple stole, kissed it and put it back in my pocket.

Shene patted my shoulder as we walked out of the chapel.

'That was a lovely thing you did for Dad, Mark. You know, he was proud of you, he really was. He just didn't know how to tell you.'

I just wanted to get out into the fresh air. Lesley was there – she flung her arms round me, kissed me on the cheek and whispered, 'I love you' into my ear. 'I love you too,' I said, and held her for a moment. The twin boys she was carrying would never know what it was like to be unloved and unwanted, I promised myself at that moment.

As I stood waiting outside the crematorium for the funeral cortege to arrive, at least I felt I looked the part in my clerical robes. The honour guard from the Burma Star Association assembled, looking very smart in their blazers, berets and white gloves. A couple of women came over to talk to me, asking who I was.

'Oh, so you're Billy's son,' one of them said. 'He always used to say he had a son who was a priest, but we weren't sure whether to believe him or not. He used to tell some tall tales. Looks like he was right about you, though.' As they went in to take their seats I heard them say, 'Fancy that! Billy's son a priest!'

My brother Paul arrived, accompanied by someone from his church who'd driven him over and was acting as his minder. He looked very nervy and unsure of himself. We hugged and he went inside.

Finally the funeral car and the hearse arrived, with my sisters Shene and Jenny and their husbands. I processed into the crematorium in front of Dad's coffin, reading aloud the words from the Bible: 'Jesus said, "I am the Resurrection and the Life. He who believes in me shall never die." We brought nothing into the world; we take nothing out. Blessed are those who mourn, for they shall be comforted.'

As I waited at the lectern, the coffin was placed onto its stand. I looked out across the array of faces. It was surreal - they all knew Dad better than I did. I'd found out more about him last night than I'd ever known before.

Everything went off better than I'd expected. There were some tears, but some laughs too, especially when I told the cigarette story. It felt strange to refer to Dad by his Christian name, something I'd never done before. I was thankful when we reached the act of committal and the Burma Star representatives stood to attention and raised the standard. I turned to face the coffin and said, 'We have entrusted William Edwards to God's merciful keeping and now we commit his body to be cremated, earth to earth, dust to dust, ashes to ashes, in sure and certain hope of the resurrection to eternal life through our Lord, Jesus Christ, who died, was buried and rose again for us...' I pressed the button and the curtains began to close. The standard was lowered and the Last Post played. I closed my eyes and prayed for a little more strength to give the final blessing.

As I predicted, Paul went completely to pieces and had to be helped out of the crematorium. Bless him, he couldn't help it. I felt exactly the same – emotionally drained, but like a volcano that could explode at any moment. However, I had a job to do and a role to live up to, so there was no time for grief.

Still dressed in my cassock, I mingled among the guests at the buffet in Dad's residential home. Everyone said what a lovely service it had been, but I just wanted the day to be over.

By the time Lesley and I had collected the children from Fram's house and driven back to Barrow, it had been dark for hours. Lesley opted for the spare room, where she was more likely to get a decent night's sleep. I lay awake, too wound up to relax, going through the events of the day in my mind. And then the tears started to flow.

'Oh God, where are you when it hurts?' I wondered. Despite my ministry and my calling as a priest, I didn't feel I had an answer to that question any more. My faith had become so fragile. I only picked up the Bible as a tool to be used, not as a book to read in order to find God. But no one need know how much I was struggling. I had a ready-made role to fill and I knew I could do it, like I had today. I'd carry on taking services, preaching sermons, visiting and marrying and burying my parishoners, and hiding the growing hollowness I felt inside. But tonight I lay alone in the dark, weeping for my dad.

*

Although I was still struggling with my own faith, the life and work of the church continued. Not even Lesley knew how difficult I was finding wrestling with my inner demons. Behind closed doors I was getting desperate. I tried everything I could to rekindle the flame of faith: I used prayer books, read books about others who had struggled with their faith, and said both morning and evening prayer religiously. I appreciated the discipline of the daily office – especially after I'd learnt to fit it in when I was most awake. I often did not say morning prayer until 10 o'clock, and evening prayer very late in the evening. I faithfully led worship and ministered to my flock, hoping that if I carried on doing what I was supposed to do, I'd eventually get through this dry and arid time.

I was frustrated with myself. I really did want to live a life pleasing to God, and in the service of others. The only way I felt able to achieve it was through becoming task orientated. I kept myself busy, attending meetings and listening to endless talks on how the church needed to engage with ordinary people outside its doors. A lot of what was said seemed to me to be irrelevant. What people need is to hear about a loving God who is interested in them and their lives, and who accepts them just as they are, not a whole line of religious hoops to jump through. For me, mission meant getting out among the people of the Ormsgill estate, loving and caring for them, making connections and establishing relationships. Pastoral care had always been a priority for me. It wasn't about getting bums on seats.

David, the rector, was always a shining example to me. He was a dear man, and so full of the spirit of God. I could see that he too got frustrated with endless church meetings which got hijacked by non-spiritual issues – the fabric of the building, and the disruption children were causing in the services.

Christmas was always a lovely time in the church and I was looking forward to celebrating my second Christmas at St Francis. Children played a huge part in our Christmas services. The Christingle service was a particularly special time, as we lit the candles in the Christingle oranges and sang 'Away in a manger'. All the Christmas services were well attended by people from the estate. Things got a bit rowdy from time to time, but it did my heart good to see some of the most hardened men and women from the estate in church, singing their hearts out. Midnight Mass was another lovely service, when I felt almost like a bishop, dressed in my cope with the golden tapestry. Getting home well after midnight, I sat at my desk eating the Easter egg I'd saved. My old friend Davo and I both made a habit of doing this - it reminded us of Christ's sacrifice on the cross on the day that everyone celebrates his birth. It was good to know that Davo would be sitting at his desk chomping away at his Easter egg too.

Kerry and Holly came to spend Christmas Day with us. It was Holly's birthday too, and at age five she clearly thought her birthday was a lot more important than Jesus'!

CHAPTER SIX

'Won't be long now, vicar,' said a member of the congregation cheerily as she left church one Sunday.

'How are you going to manage when the twins arrive?' wondered another lady, a Mothers' Union stalwart.

'Well, I guess we'll just get on with it,' I replied. 'It's not as though we haven't had children before.'

'Oh, but you're not spring chickens now, you know!' came the reply.

I was getting used to this sort of good-humoured exchange. Lesley and I were excited at the prospect of having the twins, but we had concerns too. Lesley was thoroughly exhausted and had taken to bed, on the doctor's advice. Jonathan and Fiona were pretty independent, which helped, and David, the rector, always enquired after Lesley and was concerned that I shouldn't overdo things. It was inevitable that I did feel under pressure, though – the demands of parish life don't conveniently disappear just because the vicar's wife is expecting twins.

The babies were due during Lent and I was conscious of the fact that if they chose to arrive during Holy Week, not only would I have a lot of services to do, but so would my colleagues who might otherwise be able to cover for me.

Kerry brought Lesley home from her latest hospital appointment just as I got back from taking my mid-week healing service.

'Well, how was it? What did they say?'

Lesley flopped down into a chair while Kerry put the kettle on.

'They say that I'm two weeks overdue and if I don't go into labour this week, they'll induce me.'

I sat on the arm of the settee and gave Lesley a hug. 'How are you feeling, love?'

'Exhausted! I'll be so glad when I'm not dragging this weight around. It does mean that Fiona is likely to miss the birth, though. Her school trip to Germany starts on Sunday.'

Fiona was so excited at the prospect of her first ever trip abroad. I knew I'd miss her and I was sure I'd be one of those irrational parents who worried about everything and nothing while she was away. When Sunday came, she bounced straight onto the coach with a quick hug for me and hardly a backward look.

'Don't forget to text me when the twins are born!' she said, and was off.

A couple of days later, I was in the garden when I heard Lesley calling from inside the house. I rushed inside to see her standing in the middle of the kitchen, her eyes damp with tears and her lip trembling.

'My waters have broken,' she said, her voice wobbling. 'I'm in labour – I've been timing the contractions.'

'Are you sure?' I said, feeling a bit stunned.

'Of course I am. Idiot!' She laughed shakily.

'What should I do? Shall I get some hot water?' I asked, panicking slightly.

'No! Just get me to the hospital, Mark!'

We were there within ten minutes and were ushered straight into the labour ward.

'Make yourselves comfortable,' said the midwife cheerfully.

Lesley was soon puffing and panting away with her legs up in the air and her modesty covered by a waterproof blanket. I felt a bit queasy, but I wanted to be there, to see the birth of my boys and to support Lesley. As labour advanced and the pain got more intense, I held Lesley's hand and found myself puffing and panting in time with her. It must've looked surreal – I was still wearing my clerical robes and dog collar. I was glad it wasn't me giving birth, I don't know how I'd have coped with the pain. It was bad enough hearing Lesley scream. I couldn't remember what it had been like when she'd had Jonathan and Fiona, it seemed such a long time ago.

Eventually the big moment arrived.

'Push, Lesley, the head's almost out,' encouraged the midwife.

Lesley took a deep breath and pushed and screamed and pushed and then one of the babies eased out in a load of fluid, just like popping a cork.

'Who's this one?' asked the midwife, scooping the baby up in a towel.

'Joshua James Edwards,' I said, with tears in my eyes.

'Keep going, Lesley, I can see the other twin's head,' the midwife said.

Lesley took an almighty breath, screamed and pushed, gripping my hand so hard that I lost all feeling in it.

Seconds later, the other twin emerged.

'And who's this?'

'Mark Antony Edwards Junior'.

I cried with joy. Lesley was crying too, and we hugged each other for a long moment.

Then we realised.

The nurses were all huddled over baby Mark. He wasn't making a sound.

'What's wrong with our baby?'

'Don't worry, we just need to clear out his airways. He's got some fluid in them.'

Seconds later, Mark was crying lustily, like his twin.

Both boys were weighed and cleaned up and swaddled, then handed to Lesley to hold while she was sewn up. Joshua weighed five pounds and Mark weighed four. They were so tiny that I was scared to hold them. But the midwife showed me how to do it and I held them one by one, looking into their little faces and feeling so proud to be a dad again. Once they were both settled at the breast, I slipped away to phone everyone and share our good news.

The rural dean answered the call just as he was getting back on the coach from a deanery day out to York. So he made an announcement from the front of the bus, and everyone erupted into cheers. He told me later it was the perfect end to a lovely day. My sisters and brothers-in-law were thrilled, as were Kerry and Holly. Fiona texted back from Germany with love and congratulations. Even Jonathan managed a 'Well done, Dad, and love to Mam.'

I went back into the ward to see Lesley as she lay there, exhausted but radiant, her two new babies suckling contentedly. It was a beautiful moment, a perfect picture painted forever on my heart. I thanked God for the safe arrival of my two boys.

*

The harsh ringing of the telephone jolted me awake. I'd gone to sleep in my chair at home, exhausted by the day's events. It was dark outside and for a moment I was disorientated. The phone kept ringing. I looked at my watch – 11.30 pm. I'd been asleep since half past eight that evening. Who could be ringing this late?

I picked up the phone.

'Mark Edwards.'

Silence from the other end.

'Hello? Mark Edwards here,' I said again.

'It's me, love,' said Lesley. She sounded odd.

'What's wrong, darling?'

'It's Mark Junior.' Now she was crying so hard she had difficulty getting the words out. 'Oh Mark, they've had to resuscitate him twice! He went purple in his cot. He stopped breathing.'

My heart started to race.

'Les, he's all right now, isn't he?'

'No, he isn't all right! There's something seriously wrong with him. Mark, pray, please pray! His oesophagus isn't joined to his stomach. He can't eat anything. And he can't breathe properly. He's got to go to the children's hospital in Liverpool for emergency surgery, otherwise he'll die!'

I sat there, alone in the dark, trying to come to terms with the news. Baby Mark. Oh no, not my baby. Please God, not my baby.

'Mark, are you still there?'

Lesley. I had to be strong for her.

'Yes, love, I'm still here.' I wanted to hug her and reassure her. I'd pray, of course I'd pray. I just hoped God was listening. 'How's baby Joshua?'

'He's fine. He's asleep. Mark?'

'Yes?'

'I love you.'

'I love you too.'

'I've got to go now, the consultant wants to talk to me about Mark Jr's surgery. You will pray, won't you?'

'Of course I will! And I'll let everyone else know so that they can pray too.'

I put the receiver down and sat for a moment, then lifted my head and prayed aloud, 'Oh God, please don't let my son die!' I put my head in my hands and wept.

Next morning, feeling exhausted and emotionally drained, I phoned as many people as I could. The sound of the doorbell interrupted my attempts to eat breakfast. I had no appetite and was anxiously waiting to hear from Lesley.

It was Kerry. She took one look at me, flung her arms around me and hugged me.

'Oh Mark, I'm so sorry,' she said.

'Thanks, Kerry. I'm sure everything'll be OK. He's getting the best possible help,' I said, trying to be positive.

'I've phoned everyone at Spring Mount and they're all praying for you and Lesley and the babies,' she said, looking me deep in the eyes.

'Thanks, that's very comforting.' I took a deep breath and composed myself. I did up the top button of my shirt and slipped in my dog collar. I gave her a weak smile.

'Thanks for coming round, Kerry. I'll be fine. I'm a priest, remember? I'm paid to believe, even when it's hard.'

'Oh, Mark, please don't go down that road! You're a human being before you're a priest, you're bloody well allowed to have feelings like the rest of us! Priest or not, I'll give you a slap if you play that game with me.'

We were interrupted by the phone ringing.

'I must get this Kerry, I'm expecting a call from Lesley.'

'OK, I'm going. I just wanted to call and say if I can do anything to help you and Lesley, just shout.' She slammed the door and was gone.

Lesley sounded very tired but less emotional as she explained that Mark Jr had been taken to Liverpool and was still in surgery. The special medical team had arrived about 2.30am and left with Mark Jr about 3.15am. He'd been in surgery since six o'clock that morning.

Dear Lesley. Joshua had been crying a lot during the night as well, so she'd been awake more or less the whole time.

'Perhaps Joshua's missing his twin,' I suggested.

'Perhaps,' sighed Lesley. 'I have to go, Mark, but I'll call you the minute I hear anything.'

Finally the news came through. The six-hour operation had been a success. Mark Jr remained in intensive care in Liverpool while Lesley and baby Joshua stayed in Furness General Hospital.

I was in the thick of all the services for Holy Week, but whenever I could I went to see Lesley. She was being kept in hospital because Joshua was so small. Since Mark Jr had been taken away, Joshua hadn't been feeding properly and had lost weight. The sleeves on his babygrow were rolled up so as not to swamp his perfect little fingers. His tiny dimple disappeared in the folds of spare material around his neck. It was heart-wrenching watching him, our joy tainted by the knowledge that his twin was still in intensive care. Lesley was worried that she wouldn't be able to bond properly with Mark Jr because of the enforced separation.

I picked Joshua up carefully, afraid I might break something, and held him to my chest. We were all longing to be reunited with his twin. We didn't feel complete without Mark Jr.

We were due to go over to Liverpool and see Mark Jr after my Palm Sunday service. I would pick Lesley and Joshua up from the hospital in Barrow, drive to Davo's in Preston, and he'd take over from there. He knew the area better than me – and anyway, my navigational skills were non-existent. I felt very emotional and I was angry with God. Why was he making baby Mark suffer? Why couldn't he just zap everything better?

Lesley broke down the minute she saw Mark Jr lying in the ventilator, with tubes up his tiny nose and coming from his chest. All we could do was watch him through the clear plastic and touch him through portholes in the sides of the ventilator, our hands encased in rubber gloves. We held Joshua up for his twin to see, but Mark Jr didn't respond. The consultant explained that Mark Jr was doing well and should be off the ventilator in a few days and able to return to the high dependency unit at Furness General in Barrow.

Tearing ourselves away to return to Barrow wasn't easy. We wanted to take baby Mark with us. He looked so small and vulnerable, trussed up with all the tubes. It seemed incredible that he could survive.

But he did. Within a week he was back at Furness General Hospital, with Lesley and Joshua close by.

I managed to get through all my Easter services – how, I don't know. I was emotionally and spiritually drained. But situations like this always bring you back to your knees in prayer, even if you feel your prayers aren't getting any higher than the ceiling.

Now that Mark Jr was improving, it was time to call Fiona in Germany. I'd been avoiding telling her how ill he was because I knew how upset she'd be. Jonathan had been great, helping at home and visiting Lesley and Joshua to give them hugs.

Fiona sounded so excited when she came to the phone, but when I told her what had been happening she starting screaming and dropped the receiver. Her teacher picked it up and I explained to him that Mark Jr was now out of danger, trying to sound convincing for Fiona's sake.

Amazingly, within four weeks, Lesley and both the twins were home. We were a family again, and it felt wonderful.

The following Sunday I preached on how God gave up his own son, Jesus, for us, while I had nearly lost my own. Lesley arrived after the service with one twin in each arm, to a round of applause from the lovely St Francis congregation.

*

Life with the twins took some adjustment. Thankfully Lesley was on maternity leave, which gave us some time to develop a routine. Jonathan and Fiona were great with the twins – even if Fiona did make a swift exit whenever a nappy needed changing! Feeding time was always fun. I loved watching the sudden transformation from screaming babies to contented suckling, to two zonked out little ones sleeping a milky sleep. Nursing two babies was very demanding for Lesley, especially as they were still very small and not putting on weight. The district nurse suggested that Lesley should extract her own milk, which would give me the chance to help with the feeding.

I was despatched to pick up the breast pump kit from the hospital. There I was, dressed in my vicar's outfit, listening carefully while the ward sister explained how to use this bizarre contraption. Just to make sure I was assimilating all the information properly, she handed me the pump and asked me to explain its use to her. I was a little confused – she had demonstrated on herself, fully clothed of course, but surely she didn't expect me to put the device on her breast? I could just imagine the headlines in the local newspaper – 'Vicar handles ward sister's breasts'. Mercifully, she indicated that I should place the extraction pump on my own chest. I was so relieved… Lesley was in hysterics when I told her later.

Starting again with new babies in our forties was hard work. But we soon adapted. The twins could sleep through anything – Fiona and Jonathan both carried on playing their music as loudly as ever, and we even put a radio in the twins' room at night to encourage them to sleep through any noises.

Lesley used to give them a feed before she went to bed, usually about nine o'clock, and would leave me two bottles in case they woke up. Then, when I went to bed in the early hours, it was her shift again. Most of the time she'd feed them and then go back to sleep in the spare room.

We soon discovered that twins are the centre of attention wherever they go. We got used to passers-by stopping and coo-ing at them. I loved it – I was so proud of my boys. The people in my parish and beyond were lovely, and we received many cards and good wishes from people who had heard about Mark Jr's difficult start in life.

One night, when they were only five weeks old and hadn't been home long, Lesley was upstairs taking care of Joshua. I was downstairs with Mark Jr. and had just put him into his chair when a rock came flying through the window, narrowly missing his head. It must've been thrown with some force, as it ripped the curtains. I don't know what must have been going through the mind of the person who threw it. It wasn't the only incident of vandalism directed against the church, and after it happened, most people felt even more moved by our recent experiences, and even more concerned to support us.

However, below the surface there were growing tensions in the life of the parish. I knew that David, the rector, and his wife had been struggling with the minority of people who were finding recent changes hard to handle. David's ministry was touching the most unlikely people and the church was fuller than it had ever been. And his wife, Irene, was having a lot of success with the children's work. Most of the congregation were very supportive of them both. But the constant drag from the people who wanted to go back to the 'good old days' was wearing David down.

My heart sank when David rang and asked if he could come round and see me. I'd worked with him for two years and he'd never done that before – he usually just popped in.

'You've come to tell me you're leaving, haven't you?' I said with a heavy sigh, when I opened the door to him.

'How did you know that?' he queried, rather sheepishly.

'It's written all over your face.' I thought he looked worn out – and defeated. 'David, I'm so sorry. But if I'm honest, I'm not surprised. They've finally driven you out.'

'Well, I wouldn't say that. Most of the people at St Matthews are lovely and supportive. It's just that there's an element who … who make things difficult, shall we say. And it's not just the church, Mark. My elderly mother is ill and we want to move to be nearer to her.' He looked down at his hands for a moment, before carrying on.

'Mark, I know this is going to put an added burden on you, and I'm sorry. There will be an interregnum and you'll have to look after both churches. You know how it is – new clergy don't pop up to order!'

'I'll be sorry to see you go, David.' I meant it. 'And besides, we've got you to thank for the twins!'

He looked surprised.

'You know – all those prayers you prayed for us!'

He smiled. 'You're very kind, Mark. You know, you've been an excellent team vicar, and you've established yourself well in Ormsgill in a short time. Everywhere I go people speak highly of you, and that's very much to your credit. You're a people person and a man of faith.'

'People person, yes, I hope so. But I'm really struggling with the whole faith and God thing at the moment, David.'

'I know, Mark. It's understandable. You and Lesley have been through such a traumatic time. But just hang in there, lad. God won't let you down, he won't forsake you.'

I envied David his confidence. Deep down I knew he was right, but I wished I could feel it too.

David wasn't leaving for a couple of months, so we agreed that he'd baptise the twins before he left.

*

The eight weeks since the twins had come home from hospital had gone so quickly. Already we were starting to notice different character traits in each of them. I was so proud of them that I used to hold them both in my arms and walk up and down the path outside the house with them. They were worth every moment of the three years it had taken to conceive them. I couldn't think of any greater joy than holding two new born babies in my arms and looking into their eyes.

But my joy at having the family together at home was to be short-lived.

After a feed, I noticed that Mark Jr seemed to be having difficulty in breathing.

'He probably just needs winding,' said Lesley, putting him over her shoulder and starting to gently pat his back.

He was sick all over her, so she popped him back into his chair while I went to get a cloth. While I was getting it, he was sick again, projecting the vomit right across the carpet. I picked up him and could see how laboured his breathing was. Then he went lifeless and floppy in my arms.

'Lesley, we need to get him to hospital! I'll call an ambulance,' I said urgently.

'No, let me take him, it'll be quicker. You stay here with Joshua.' She snatched Mark Jr from me and strapped him back into his chair. 'I'll phone you from the hospital,' she said as she rushed out of the door.

'Oh God, please let him be OK!' I prayed, trying to stay calm, but horribly scared inside. Jonathan and Fiona waited with me for Lesley to call. Little Joshua was oblivious to what was happening. In the end, I couldn't wait any longer. I asked Jonathan to look after Joshua and called a taxi to take me to the hospital.

Lesley and Mark Jr had been taken straight to the children's high dependency unit. I ran down the corridor and the minute I was let in I could see all the doctors clustered round a bed in the corner. Lesley looked up and saw me.

'He can't breathe,' she cried. 'They're trying to help him; they've got him on oxygen.'

I eased myself in between the doctors. There was baby Mark, lying in the incubator, bare chested, with tubes up his nose and his nappy smothering his entire torso. His chest was heaving with effort. I held his tiny hand while the doctors tried to get a drip into his arm. It was unbearable to watch.

A nurse gently pushed me out of the way so that the doctors could work unhindered. I held on to Lesley, who was shaking and crying into my shoulder.

'Please tell me what's happened? What's going on?' I asked.

'We're trying to find out,' said a nurse, her eyes sympathetic.

One of the doctors looked round at us. 'Mr and Mrs Edwards, your baby is struggling. His heart may not be able to take the strain; it could stop at any moment.'

It seemed as though time stood still. How do you respond to news like that? We carried on watching, tears flowing freely, as

Mark's little chest went up and down and the doctors continued to work on him.

Eventually a nurse led us away, into the waiting area. We clung on to each other and prayed.

At last a doctor came to tell us that Mark Jr was responding to treatment, but needed to stay in hospital. We were allowed back in to see him. He was hooked up to the heart monitor, had a drip in his arm, and was breathing with the aid of oxygen. We stood over him, held his little arms, and prayed for him.

Mark Jr was in hospital for ten days, with one or other of us by his side the whole time. Lesley needed to go home sometimes to look after Joshua, so we did it in shifts.

They were difficult days. Mark Jr was monitored continually, as his stats remained dangerously low. The alarm bell kept going off as they dropped still further, and he needed oxygen and nebulisers. He was diagnosed with a severe form of pneumonia.

The church held us in their prayers and David, the rector, came round to offer us support and encouragement. The doctors and nurses were wonderful and Gerald, the hospital chaplain and my faithful spiritual director since the time of my own hospital stay just after I was ordained, made sure he included the children's ward on his rounds. All we could do, like all parents of sick children, was to entrust Mark Jr to God and leave him in the hands of the professionals.

Children can be astonishingly resilient, and ten days later, Mark Jr was back at home. Reuniting him with Joshua brought tears to our eyes. The consultant had diagnosed a congenital chest problem, possibly related to the emergency surgery he'd had when he was born, and had arranged for us to have open access at the hospital. Sure enough, every six weeks or so Mark Jr went through the same routine of projectile vomiting, struggling to breathe, dehydration and lifelessness. It was scary seeing him deteriorate so quickly, but it helped that we could pick him up and rush him straight to hospital. Lesley and I got very good at recognising the signs that meant he needed immediate attention.

*

As Christian parents, Lesley and I wanted to have the twins baptised. We saw the baptismal service as a public statement of the values and faith we intended to bring them up by. Kerry and Davo were delighted to be two of the boys' god-parents. My rector, David, would take the service as one of his last official duties before leaving the parish. Nine o'clock in the morning was early, but that was the time of all our baptismal services and I certainly wasn't going to make an exception for my own children, although it did mean that some of our family and friends from other parts of the country were unable to get there. But St Francis was full, with people from the Ormsgill estate swelling the congregation as we stood together with the godparents to welcome the twins into the church family and make solemn promises to God about how we would bring them up. The church members had done us proud with the refreshments, and everyone said what a lovely occasion it was.

There was no doubt that things were changing very rapidly in my life at this time. As well having to cope with the stress and anguish of the twins' traumatic early days, Lesley and I were adjusting to life with two small babies as well as two rapidly-growing teenagers. And I was facing big changes in my professional life as well, with David leaving the parish. I always found change difficult, and I felt alone and unsupported by the church hierarchy. I knew I could always talk to Gerald, my spiritual director, and I trusted him implicitly. But I believed that, as a priest, I should have the answers to the difficult questions of life and faith. It was my job: the profession I'd chosen and to which I was proud to belong. I was paid to believe. But inside I felt scared and insecure. There was no way I felt capable of running two churches. David had done a fantastic job at St Matthews, but I wasn't him. I'd do my best to carry through the changes he'd made, some of which hadn't been popular, and of course I'd look after St Matthews and its congregation, but St Francis and the Ormsgill estate were bound to remain my first priority. I knew there were some people who wouldn't like that – and who wouldn't like me.

And, as if that weren't enough, we were about to move house. Finally, after more than two years, St Francis house was ready for us, right opposite the church and just two miles away from the curate's house in Park Drive where we'd lived for four years. The twins' new bedroom was painted blue, with a Winnie the Pooh motif. Fiona had gone for purple, with a purple carpet. Jonathan had chosen dark green, but only because we wouldn't let him have black! He was going through a Goth phase and starting to look more like a vampire than a vicar's son. Although we didn't approve, we felt it was important to allow him to express himself, provided his school work and general behaviour weren't affected – he was only trying to find his own identity. He was a good kid. Sometimes I didn't handle him very well, I'd fly off the handle and be confrontational. Lesley was much better at remaining calm and letting him have his own space. I loved all my children but I was so afraid of being a bad father. The truth was, I had no role model to look up to, and my own inadequacies as a parent sometimes reduced me to tears.

Lesley had finished maternity leave and gone back to work, and the interregnum began better than I'd feared. With the help of the retired clergy who lived in the parish I was able to keep my promise to David and retain both the new, informal family service and the traditional service at St Matthew's.

It had been a bit of a surprise during this time to discover that we'd had a visit from an undercover journalist from the Northwest Evening Mail during a service. Much to my delight, her experience was a positive one. She rated every aspect at least eight out of ten, with nine out of ten for the sermon, relevance, accessibility and good for children. And said she'd been made to feel very welcome and had left feeling uplifted.

*

Our first Christmas in our new home was memorable for all the wrong reasons. The house looked lovely, and the twins were entranced by the baubles twinkling on the Christmas tree in the living room. Lying on their backs, they would throw their hands in the air trying to catch the pretty things and gurgling with delight.

A week before Christmas, with the Christingle service, the carol services, Midnight Mass and the Christmas Day service itself on my mind, I was in my study when I heard Lesley shout down from upstairs.

'Mark, come up! Something's wrong with Mark Jr!'

I rushed upstairs but by the time I reached the top Mark Jr had already gone floppy in Lesley's arms. He'd been vomiting and was struggling to breathe. I pulled back his vest and could see that his chest was still moving, but the breaths looked frighteningly laboured. I held him to my chest and he was sick down my back.

'He needs to get to hospital immediately,' I told Lesley, grateful that we had open access. 'You take him, I'll look after Joshua.'

Mark Jr was admitted straight to the high dependency unit, barely conscious, with pneumonia. Lesley stayed with him while I did my best to run both parishes. There was simply no one else around who could step into the breach. All the services in both churches carried on as usual. I even had to take a funeral, all the time wondering if Mark Jr was going to make it. So far, he wasn't responding to treatment, but just lay still, hooked up to monitors, with tubes and drips giving him food and oxygen. It was just like before. All we could do was watch and pray, and try not to panic every time the alarms went off when his stats dropped.

I was so proud of my family. Lesley was being a real tower of strength, and it was lovely to see Jonathan trying to support me and Fiona, who was distraught. Friends from both churches and the Ormsgill estate prayed and called with messages of support.

By Christmas morning, the news was better. Mark Jr was beginning to respond, but he wouldn't be out of hospital until after the holiday. In fact, he was the only baby in the hospital on Christmas Day. The photographer from the Northwest Evening Mail came and took his picture, looking cute and angelic sitting between the legs of a huge stuffed reindeer.

CHAPTER SEVEN

I welcomed the New Year in by myself in 2003. Mark Jr was back at home and he and Joshua were peacefully asleep, undisturbed by the whizzes and bangs of the Barrow fireworks. Lesley was at work, Jonathan was out with his mates, and Fiona had gone to bed. I stood staring into the night sky, wondering what the new year would bring. The old year had certainly been a challenging one.

Two things happened in the early months of 2003 which resulted in key relationships being formed and my ministry expanding in unusual areas.

For almost three years I'd been campaigning to have a community police officer appointed to the Ormsgill estate. The vast majority of the people I talked to on the estate told me again and again that they would like to have a community officer permanently stationed in the heart of the community.

Late one evening, there was a ring at the door bell. I'd been dozing on a bean bag in front of the television, Lesley was in bed, the twins had just had a late bottle and were settled, and Jonathan and Fiona were both in their rooms. Outside, I could hear the wind howling and rain lashing against the window pane. 'Who on earth is mad enough to be out in this weather at this time of night?' I wondered.

I dragged myself upright and looked through the spy hole in the front door. A police officer was standing there, rainwater running off his helmet and onto his face. I wondered what on earth he could want.

I opened the door. 'Hello constable, what can I do for you on this godforsaken night?'

'I'm PC 153 Ollie Hamilton,' he said, in a deep Scottish accent. 'I'm the new community officer for Ormsgill, I'm soaked to the skin and I'm fed up. The Chief Superintendant has sent me to make contact with you.'

His introduction was typical of PC Ollie – blunt and to the point. He was a large, stocky man, in his early thirties: a proper street copper. I immediately had a feeling we were going to get on.

'Aren't you going to ask me in, Father?' He wiped the rain from his eyes.

'Sorry! Yes, of course, do come in!'

He stepped inside and took off his helmet.

'Look at the state of me! I shouldn't be out on a night like this without a car. I don't think the Chief Super likes me very much,' he growled.

'Well, I don't think the archdeacon likes me very much, so we've got something in common, haven't we?' I replied.

'Aye lad, that we do! Have you got the fire on? I want to dry out before I go back to the nick.'

Before I had time to reply, he was shrugging off his sodden jacket and utility belt.

'And you'll be putting the kettle on, Father, no doubt,' he added.

'Please call me Mark!' I said over my shoulder as I showed him into the study and headed for the kitchen.

'OK – and you can call me Ollie. Do you mind if I take my boots off?'

Jonathan and Fiona appeared at the top of the stairs, looking worried.

'Dad!' Jonathan whispered. 'What does that copper want?'

'Why, what have you done?' I teased. 'It must be something bad to make a copper turn out in this weather. Have you been smoking those happy cigarettes again?'

It later turned out that that's exactly what he had been doing. If I'd known at the time, I would never have joked about it. A tearful confession later to Lesley resulted in him never touching the stuff again.

'Come on Dad,' piped up Fiona. 'What's he really doing here?'

'Calm down, both of you. He's come to see me, not you. He's PC Ollie, the new community officer for the estate.'

When I returned to the study with a steaming mug of tea for PC Ollie and coffee for myself, my visitor was sitting comfortably on the settee, his feet stretched out, warming his socks by the gas fire.

'Feeling better, constable?'

'Aye. It's a wild night, make no mistake.' He took a sip of tea, then coughed and spat it out.

'What's the matter?' I asked.

'I canna drink this, lad. It's awful weak. What sort of tea bags does your wife buy?'

'Decaf.'

'I can't stand decaf. Haven't you got anything else?'

I shook my head, smiling. By now I knew we were going to be friends.

'Give me your mug,' I held out my hand for it. 'I'll see what I can do.'

Back in the kitchen I put two decaf tea bags into Ollie's mug, left them a good long while, then squeezed them hard.

'How's that?' I asked, handing him back the mug.

'Hmm. It'll do. What biscuits have you got?'

PC Ollie stayed a couple of hours, drying out, sipping tea and chatting. It turned out that he'd actually volunteered for the position of community officer on the Ormsgill estate. He'd only been in the area a short time, having moved from Dundee with his wife and two young children, but they were settling in well.

I was pleased that my campaign had eventually paid off. What I did not know, until much later, was that the Chief Superintendant had not just asked PC Ollie to go and see the vicar, he'd asked him to keep me on a leash – preferably a tight one!

PC Ollie agreed that I could go out with him on the beat as he started getting to know his new patch. He knew, as I did, that although most of Ormsgill were keen to see him, there was an element on the estate that didn't take kindly to any authority figures. And some people resented the fact that community policing had been withdrawn back in the 1970s and they felt abandoned as a result. Now, though, it was good to see PC Ollie move into the substation – a small office right next to the post office, in the parade of shops at the heart of the estate. Ollie raided local skips for abandoned furniture to make the place useable, and soon began to build relationships with people in the community. He was so often seen out and about with me, and we so often appeared side by side in the local newspaper, that he was known as 'God's cop' by his colleagues.

Within two years, he'd made such an impact that he received a Good Policing award from the Chief Constable. I was delighted, and invited the Chief Constable, along with people from the estate, to a special celebration at the vicarage. It was the first time anything like this had ever happened in the community. Ollie's old office furniture was replaced with new in time for the Chief's inspection. I had special police signs made to go on his office wall, a new name plaque for his desk, and a blue police light for the outside of the substation. It looked really good!

On the day of the presentation, PC Ollie and I waited together outside the vicarage for the Chief Constable to arrive. Ollie was pacing up and down like a cat on a hot tin roof. He was so nervous that he was making me nervous too.

'Ollie, will you settle down!' I urged. 'You're making me restive. I've been to the loo three times already.'

'How's my salute?' Ollie asked me in response, snapping his white-gloved hand up to the saluting position.

'Just fine, Constable,' I laughed.

Soon enough, the big black Range Rover drew up and the driver got out, holding the door open for the Chief.

PC Ollie saluted, shook hands with his boss, and introduced me.

'Nice to meet you, Father Mark. I've heard a lot about you,' said the Chief Constable. 'I do want to thank you for your support for all my officers, Constable Hamilton in particular.'

'It's a pleasure, Chief Constable. Do come this way, Chief Constable, and meet some representatives from the estate.'

'Lead the way!'

'Thank you, Chief Constable. Follow me, Chief Constable.'

As we walked in, I felt a kick on the heel of my shoe. PC Ollie was trying to get my attention.

'Stop it, Mark!' he hissed.

'What? What am I doing?'

'You don't have to call him 'Chief Constable' every second, you idiot!'

'Oh … thanks, constable!'

When we got indoors I invited the Chief Constable to say a few words.

'Certainly, Father Mark,' he replied. 'But please do call me Mike, you don't have to keep addressing me as Chief Constable!'

'Told you, lad!' grinned Ollie.

The visit was a great success. It was a tribute to PC Ollie's good work, but it was also a real morale boost to a community which had had its fair share of troubles and believed that no one cared.

I loved my involvement with the police service, not just in Ormsgill but in the wider community in Barrow-in-Furness. To me, being a priest wasn't just about what I did in church on Sunday, it was about relating faith and belief to daily life. I always maintained that if Jesus was physically with us today, he wouldn't be stuck in a building but would be walking the length and breadth of the country, engaging with people wherever he met them. I tried to be like that: I'd always stop and chat to people, even when I was meant to be helping Lesley with the supermarket shopping. Lesley soon got used to leaving me chatting in the aisles while she zipped about with the trolley.

But behind closed doors, my struggle with my own relationship with God was getting worse. I did a lot of religious things and followed lots of rituals, but my soul ached for the passion I once knew. What had happened? Here I was, living my dream of serving God, yet somehow the exhilaration and excitement had drained away. I was even jealous of friends who'd come to faith under my ministry. People like Kerry, whose passion for Jesus reminded me of what my own relationship with him used to be like. I'm not saying I wasn't pious, or sincere – I was both – but, try as I might, I couldn't bring that close personal relationship back. I was empty and lonely inside. And I was scared. I was beginning to wonder how long I could carry on as a priest. If I had to abandon the priesthood, what would I do? How would I be able to provide for my family?

*

I was flicking through my local paper, the North West Evening Mail, when a headline caught my eye: 'Duddon Inshore Rescue takes delivery of rescue vehicle.' I'd never heard of Duddon Inshore Rescue, but I learnt that they were based in Askam in Furness, a remote village on the edge of the Duddon estuary. The article, which was about the water company donating a Land Rover which had been converted into a mobile response unit, was interesting, but it was the final sentence which made my heart leap. They were looking for volunteers.

I'd been chaplain of the local RNLI for some while, and felt privileged to be able to visit the life-boat station and chat to the brave volunteers. But it was clear that not everyone was happy about my presence, and I was disappointed when my request to join the crew had been refused. Although the rejection hurt, it didn't stop me from dreaming about going out on the boat and rescuing people.

But perhaps I could join Duddon Inshore Rescue instead? Maybe they wouldn't mind having a vicar in their crew? I would love to be able to do something really worthwhile – and it would be a welcome distraction from the difficulties in the church and my crisis of faith.

I was just reaching out my hand to make the call, when Lesley shouted for me from upstairs. It was Mark Jr again, having another attack. We were familiar with the routine by now, but it still made my heart lurch seeing Lesley bundle Mark Jr up and rush him to the hospital, leaving me at home with Joshua.

It seemed like an age before she rang.

'He's in intensive care again,' she told me. 'The consultant says he's in danger of cardiac arrest, his heart is under so much strain.'

Mark Jr was semi-conscious, and hooked up once again to drips and oxygen, but fighting hard. It was always emotionally and physically draining when he was in hospital. A long waiting game, punctuated by alarm bells going off, doctors and nurses coming and going, different drugs being pumped into him in the hope that one would work, and all the time watching and hoping for some improvement in his condition. The consultants and paediatricians were wonderful, but even they had to admit at times that they were baffled by Mark Jr's sudden deteriorations and recoveries.

During the day, Lesley and I took it in turns to stay with him. She was able to take compassionate leave from work for most of the time, but as Mark's health problems continued she had to start using up her holiday entitlement.

At night, Lesley slept in a put-up bed beside Mark Jr's hospital cot, while I took care of Joshua at home. It tore at my heartstrings when I put Joshua to bed and looked across at Mark's empty cot on the other side of the room.

But life had to go on. I kept going with my parish duties, and never missed saying morning and evening prayer, however flat and uninspired they felt. At least going through the motions kept some sort of channel open between me and God – or that's what I hoped. But the constant worry about losing Mark Jr was like a dead weight dragging me down and constantly hijacking my thoughts. I know I got impatient with some of the trivial bickering in the church and all the discussions about the 'right' way of doing things. What did personality clashes and religious traditions matter when my son's life was so fragile? Deep down, I believed that Jesus didn't care too much about religious traditions either.

At last, Mark Jr began to improve. As he recovered it was lovely to see him sitting up, taking an interest in his surroundings, and charming the nurses. At nearly one year old he could say the odd word and loved to wave his hands around and point at anything that caught his eye. He was also very good at throwing things and you soon learned to duck when he had something in his hands. He was no respecter of persons, as the consultant discovered when Mark Jr threw a toy at him then grabbed his stethoscope.

It was interesting to watch Mark Jr and Joshua when we brought Mark Jr home. Stroking each others' faces and making cute little noises, they were obviously pleased to be together again. All the emotional strain that Lesley had been under suddenly came to the surface and she burst into tears. We'd been through so much as a family. All I wanted to do was hold Lesley close and watch my sleeping babies.

When Lesley was back at work and everything was returning to normal in St Francis house, I picked up the newspaper cutting which still lay on my desk. Would the Duddon Inshore Rescue service still need volunteers, several weeks later? Well, there was only one way to find out. I dialled the number and waited.

'Hello, Dave Caldwell here.'

'Ah, hello Dave. My name's Mark Edwards. I read your article in the paper and wonder if you still need volunteers for Duddon Inshore Rescue?'

'Yes, we certainly do!'

'Oh, great. Good.' I took a deep breath. I didn't want to be rejected again, like I had been with the RNLI. 'Um, I'm very interested in joining, but I'm a vicar. Will that matter?'

'Shouldn't think so. It'll have to be put to a committee meeting, but I don't see why it should be a problem.'

To my delight, Dave suggested that I meet him at the boathouse on Sunday afternoon so that he could show me around. I couldn't wait.

*

I did my normal two Sunday morning services at St Francis then had an hour to kill before the 11 o'clock service at St Matthews. I was getting increasingly concerned that numbers at the 11 o'clock service had been dwindling since David, the rector, had left. I had kept the promise I'd made to him to keep the service going, despite considerable pressure to reunite the two services. But it was difficult. The music, in particular, was a struggle. I wanted little Ellie, the St Francis organist, to play at St Matthews, but I was talked out of that idea, against my better judgment. So the few faithful attendees at the 11 o'clock service had to make do with CDs to sing along to. Sometimes it was OK, but often it just didn't work. It was disheartening seeing people drift away and not feeling able to stop them.

I was glad when I was able to escape from parish concerns and drive through the darkening February afternoon to Askam, five miles from Ormsgill. As arranged, I waited for Dave Caldwell outside the Co-op. I immediately recognised his blue Ford Focus when it pulled up – the blue reflective strip in the rear window with the words 'Emergency Rescue Vehicle' was a dead giveaway. 'Wow, I'd love one of those!' was my first thought. Another strip bore the words 'H M Coastguard'.

Dave was a blond man in his late twenties. He was station officer and chairman of Duddon Inshore Rescue as well as a crew member for the coastguard. He sounded surprised when I told him I was the RNLI chaplain.

'Couldn't you join the RNLI crew?' he asked.

'I'd love to, but they won't let me,' I explained.

'Why not?'

'Apparently I live too far away from the RNLI station,' I said, telling him the reason I'd been given. It had never seemed likely to me, but I felt I should accept it with good grace.

'That's bollocks!' Dave exclaimed. 'I know half the crew and most of them work in Barrow and would have just as far to travel as you for a day-time call out.'

I loved his colourful language - and I knew he was right.

'Yeah. I've just had to accept that that's their policy. But actually I think it's more to do with the fact that I'm a vicar. I've been told that it wouldn't go down well with some of the existing crew if a vicar or a woman were to join.' Despite my disappointment, I still had the highest regard for the bravery of the RNLI crew. I just wished I could've joined them, that was all.

By now, we'd driven through the village and down a dirt track past some allotments. There in front of us was the boat house, with blue double doors and 'Life Boat, Keep Clear' painted on them in huge letters. A plaque commemorated its opening in 1969, when I would have been nine years old. Inside stood the big blue tractor, 'Old Blue' as it was known, with the 5.75 metre orange rib boat behind it.

'Well this is it. What do you think?' asked Dave.

I was in awe. 'Very impressive,' I said, inadequately.

Dave gave me a potted history of the station, which had been set up following a series of deaths by drowning of local people. The local vicar at the time had been part of the original committee that was set up to consider the possibility of starting a rescue service to cover the Duddon Estuary. Around the walls hung testimonies to the more than 400 call outs the station had responded to since its opening. Just a few months ago, Dave and another crew member had swum out to rescue a local woman who was caught up in flood water and in danger of being swept away. They had both received bravery awards for their efforts.

I was having the time of my life. We saw the crew room, the new mobile response unit, the quad bike, complete with blue light, even the drying room where all the crew's kit was hanging. Then up the stairs to the tower where the radio comms, log books, maps, binoculars, charts and incident logs were kept. The station was functional and well equipped but not grand, and I was interested when Dave told me that they received no state or other funding but had to raise all the money they needed themselves.

I couldn't wait to be a part of all this.

'How soon will you be able to let me know if the committee has agreed to me joining?' I asked, trying not to sound too keen.

'Well, our next meeting happens to be next week,' said Dave. 'Once it's agreed, I can give you a pager, but you'll need to be a crew member for six months before you get your uniform.'

'Uniform?'

'Yeah – white shirt with epaulettes, tie, jumper with your name and life boat embroidery on it, polo shirt, fleece and baseball cap. You have to buy your own black trousers.'

Oh wow, I thought, this gets better and better! I really like uniforms.

As Dave continued to explain the set-up at Duddon, he began opening up a bit about himself too. He was recently divorced, and spoke passionately about the pain of only seeing his two small children at weekends. I came to know him as a very caring and sensitive man, with a real pastoral heart towards the Duddon crew. He hadn't been chairman or station officer long, although he had been part of the crew for nine years. Dave promised I'd soon meet his predecessor, Bernard McNamee, a local legend.

By the time Dave dropped me back at my car, my head was spinning. Just before he drove off into the February darkness, he said something I've never forgotten. 'Mark, you'll get out of the organisation what you're prepared to put into it.' I knew he was right.

'So, how did it go?' Lesley gave me a quick hug as I walked into the kitchen.

'Fantastic!' I barely paused for breath as I told her about everything I'd seen and heard. When I finally ran out of steam, I thought she didn't appear to be quite as excited as I thought she should be. She looked at me.

'Mark, promise me one thing.'

'What? Aren't you pleased?'

'Yes, of course – but promise me you won't go over the top.'

'What ever do you mean?'

'Oh, come on, you know you've got a bit of an obsessive personality. Once you decide you're going to do something, you do tend to take it to extremes.'

'When have I ever done that?' I was most indignant.

'Oh dear.' She shook her head. 'Where do I begin…?'

Secretly, I knew she was right. Once I'd committed to something, it was all or nothing. I couldn't help it. It was just the way I was.

Later that evening, after I'd changed the twins' nappies, given them their bottles, played with them a bit, then settled them down for the night, I showered and changed, then relaxed with Lesley, leaning against the bean bag watching Heartbeat on television.

'We should go there for a mini break,' suggested Lesley, dreamily. 'It looks lovely.'

I was just starting to tell her all the reasons why it wouldn't be lovely, when the babies started crying upstairs. Fiona bellowed down, 'Muuum! The twins are crying!'

'Probably need clean nappies,' I suggested, helpfully.

Lesley looked at me. I looked at Lesley. She rolled her eyes upwards, in a hinting sort of way.

'No way! I put them to bed! Your turn, my dear.' I pretended to concentrate on the TV screen.

'Muuuum! Daaaaad! I'm TRYING to do my HOMEWORK!'

Lesley sighed, rolled off the beanbag and crawled to the door, using the handle to pull herself up…

I settled back into the beanbag, feeling content and grateful to God for my family. It would be lovely to have a break together. Maybe Goatland, where Heartbeat was filmed, wasn't such a bad idea as a holiday destination after all.

*

A couple of weeks went by and I was starting to get worried. I still hadn't heard from Dave Caldwell. I was beginning to convince myself that the life boat committee had voted against me because I was a vicar. Even after years in the ministry I hadn't really come to terms with the variety of ways in which people reacted to my profession. I'd always thought that being a clergyman – dedicating your life to serving God and serving people – was a noble profession. But clearly not everyone shared that view. Some people immediately assumed I was out to convert them. Others resented or felt threatened by the dog collar and seemed to need to put on a show in front of me. Some people just plain disliked anyone who stood up for decent morals and a positive view of religion. I was starting to feel that if I wore a studded collar and nose rings I'd come across less prejudice than I did when wearing a clerical collar.

'Don't worry. It's only been a couple of weeks.' Lesley stroked my bald head reassuringly. 'You're so impatient.'

At that precise moment the doorbell rang and Lesley jumped off my knee to answer it.

A smiling Dave Caldwell followed her back into my study.

'Hi Mark. I've just dropped in to bring you your pager.'

'You mean the committee said yes?' I could feel a huge grin starting to spread all over my face.

'Yup. A unanimous decision.'

'Wow!' I was genuinely moved. They wanted me! My dream had come true. I could be part of a life boat crew at last.

'Told you to be patient, didn't I?' smirked Lesley. 'He'd convinced himself you didn't want him because he's a priest,' she explained to Dave.

'Not at all! We accept volunteers from all walks of life,' he added, with a chuckle.

'What happens now?' I wanted to know.

'You're officially on call from this moment. Training takes place every Monday down at the station, plus a couple of Sundays per month. Sometimes there's extra training, which we'll page you about. So when your pager goes off, it won't necessarily be a call out.'

'Sundays could be difficult for me sometimes. Will that matter?'

'No, just come when you can. The training involves just about everything we do – tractor driving, radio work, search and rescue map reading, first aid, quad biking, helming the boat. At first, if you happen to be one of the first to arrive, you'll go out as an observer.'

I was so excited I could barely concentrate on what he was saying. Before he left, Dave told me that my call sign and crew number would be Duddon 16. He also suggested that I consider sitting on the committee, as I was already on the RNLI committee. I wasn't sure if sitting on both would be seen as a conflict of interests, but I was more than happy to do the work if I was allowed to.

The following Sunday, I was sitting in my study reflecting on the two morning services I'd just taken. They'd both been baptismal services, one at St Francis and one at St Matthews. I'd enjoyed both of them – the baptismal parties from both families had been lively and responsive during the services, and had both made lovely comments afterwards about how much they'd enjoyed them. It made me feel good to know that they felt welcomed and comfortable in my churches, and I was pleased that everything had gone smoothly.

My positive thoughts were interrupted by a beeping noise. I leant over to my computer, pressed a few keys and twiddled the connections. The beeping continued. 'What's Jonathan been up to this time?' I wondered, crossly. He was always getting into trouble for using my computer and messing things up.

Suddenly it dawned on me. It wasn't the computer – it was my pager!

I unclipped it from my belt and looked at the screen.

'Immediate launch, Liverpool Coast Guard,' it read.

I raced through the house, shouting, 'I've got to go! Someone's in trouble!'

I drove to the boat house as fast as I could within the speed limit, flashing my headlights at other drivers and pulling down the blue Rescue visor on the passenger side of the car. I could feel the adrenaline pumping and felt breathless with nerves and excitement.

When I arrived at the boat house I saw that the big blue doors were already open and the boat and tractor were on their way down to be launched from the beach. I parked quickly, then raced upstairs to the tower.

'Hi, I'm the new boy. What can I do?' Ian, one of the training officers, was already manning the radio. Darren, the other training officer, had been dispatched with the boat, along with Trevor the helmsman and Keith as radio operator.

The radio crackled into life.

'Duddon Base, Duddon Base, Duddon IRB, Duddon IRB.'

'Duddon IRB, Duddon Base, go ahead, over,' responded Ian.

'Duddon Base, Duddon IRB, casualty has been recovered from the water and is in the boat. We are returning to shore, south side of Askam pier. Request mobile response unit and first officer meet us at the shore line, over.'

'I heard that,' said Dave Caldwell, who'd just arrived. 'I'll take the mobile unit with Peter. Mark, would you like to get some kit on? You can come with us.'

I rushed to the locker room, where I met Peter getting into his flotation suit. I scrambled into a spare suit and we each grabbed a hard hat before climbing into the land rover and setting off at speed, lights flashing and siren on, for Askam pier.

An hour later, I was back in the boathouse with the rest of the crew for our debrief. The casualty had been safely recovered, taken to hospital, checked over and released, Dave told us.

'Thank you all for responding,' said Dave. 'A good turnout, and job well done. Now, for those of you who don't know him, can I introduce Father Mark, our newest recruit? Some of you have probably seen him in the Evening Mail!'

There was some friendly laughter.

'Mark is chaplain for the RNLI and vicar of St Francis in Ormsgill,' explained Dave.

'Ormsgill! That's a rough place, and no mistake!' said one of the crew.

'It's not that bad!' I was always ready to defend my patch.

'Hmm… I heard it was twinned with Beirut!' joked someone else.

Everyone laughed again and I knew I'd feel at home in this group of men.

CHAPTER EIGHT

March 23, 2003, was a special day. The twins were a year old. It was a day of celebration as we looked back over their first year of life and gave thanks to God for entrusting us with these precious children.

Jonathan and Fiona came into the twins' bedroom to help them open their presents, Fiona in her school uniform, and Jonathan in his normal Goth get-up of dyed black hair, pale make-up and false eye covers. I would not let him peep inside the twins' cots looking like that – he scared me, never mind them! He was a good lad: a bit confrontational and sullen from time to time, but he responded well to Lesley's calm approach to parenting, and sometimes even acted as peacemaker between me and Fiona. Any fireworks were often due to me losing my temper as I tried to impose my authority on him.

Fiona was the more stressy personality, especially now that she was a teenager. She was a real drama queen and for her everything was a major crisis. I was also beginning to suspect that she was experimenting with alcohol. Lesley and I were both teetotal, but we had given permission for Jonathan at sixteen to have an occasional glass of wine when out for a meal with friends. Recently I'd found an empty bottle hidden behind the blinds in the kitchen, and I had a feeling that Fiona was the culprit. I was ready to go off the deep end, but Lesley promised to have a word with Fiona about the dangers of drinking and the fact that she was under age.

Now, though, it was a joy to see big brother and big sister getting down on the floor with the twins and helping them rip the paper off their presents, even if the twins seemed more interested in tearing the paper than playing with their new toys! Despite the hard work of having two babies to look after, not to mention all the dreadful uncertainties about Mark Jr's health, the twins were a real blessing to us. I just hoped that I'd be a good father to them. I already felt inadequate as the parent of two teenagers, and in my worst moments I was convinced that all my children would end up hating me.

Later that day, Davo came over from Preston to help us celebrate, and Kerry arrived with Holly and some more presents.

We had a great evening, although I had to rescue Davo, who had retreated to my study for a quiet read of the paper, from being jumped on by Holly.

*

I loved being part of the crew of Duddon Inshore Rescue, and was finding it a real relief from some of the problems of daily life. When I arrived at the boathouse I could simply be myself.

I was a regular at the training sessions and had been thrilled to be allowed to have a go at driving the tractor, the quad bikes and the mobile response ambulance. I was even allowed to take the helm of the rib, under supervision. My radio training was coming on and I no longer felt so nervous when talking to base or the Liverpool Coast Guard.

The crew had taken me to their hearts and I felt accepted by them. There were some interesting characters among them, and relationships were sometimes a bit difficult, which was only to be expected in a small, closely-knit group of people. I sensed some tensions between the old Askam crew and some of the newer members who, like me, lived outside the village. Dave himself, although a brilliant head of station, fell into the latter group and occasionally felt slightly unsure of his position around some of the older and more long-serving crew members. I found Trevor particularly difficult, but we did have a lot of fun together. I'll never forget the joke he played on me during the foot and mouth crisis in Cumbria. I'd just returned to the boat house in my reflective waterproofs and Wellingtons, having been down on the shoreline as part of the ground crew. I noticed a bowl of water and disinfectant standing outside the door, but ignored it, at that stage not knowing why it was there, and continued towards the crew room, only to be met by shouts from Trevor and Keith to go back and stand in it and wash my boots. I dutifully obliged and stood there for ages scrubbing my boots while Trevor watered me with the hosepipe. Very thoroughly. In fact, so thoroughly that I was wet through to my skin by the time I stepped out of the bowl and sloshed off to change.

One of the biggest characters was Dave's predecessor as head of station, Bernard McNamee. Bernard, a founding member, had lived and breathed inshore rescue for more than 40 years. The first time I met him, at a committee meeting, he sat there in his immaculate black and white uniform, with a very grand gold insignia on his shoulders, not saying a word. I later discovered that the gold braid was homemade and had started life as curtain cord! As I got to know him better, I grew to love and appreciate Bernard. I helped him to get an MBE for services to the community but I always rather envied him and used to joke that I'd take his funeral if I could have his braided hat and medal. Bernard commanded both respect and affection but was far more than just an authority figure. He was a law unto himself, and his wife, Margaret, despaired of him. She'd often call the boat house, looking for him, and we'd have to pretend he'd just left and was on his way home. One particular day, Margaret rang up to tell us that Bernard really wasn't well and shouldn't be doing anything strenuous.

'It's OK, Margaret,' I said, 'he's just watching the rest of us work.'

When I came off the phone I shouted up to Bernard, 'You'll catch it if Margaret comes in and sees you, you old sea dog!' He was perched precariously at the top of a ladder, drilling holes in the wall in order to remount the honours plaque, which weighed a ton. Bernard just laughed and carried on.

After six months with Duddon Inshore Rescue, Dave handed me the box with my uniform in it. I could not wait to go home to try it on and show it to Lesley.

'Here I come, ready or not,' I announced from the bathroom. Lesley was lying on our bed, watching television.

I made my entrance and she went quiet for a moment. Then she got up, threw her arms round my neck and pushed me down onto the bed.

'Hmm, you're not the only one who likes a uniform,' she murmured, attacking the buttons.

Before things got really interesting, we were interrupted by wailing from the twins' room. Lesley laughed and lay still on top of me. The wailing got louder.

'Oh well. I'd better go or they'll wake up Jonathan and Fiona.' She eased herself off the bed, did up her clothes and made her way to the door.

'So you like the uniform, then?' I asked.

'What do you think?' She teased me with a flash of thigh as she left the room.

Thanks to Lesley's skills with money, we were eventually able to save up enough to have a two week break in Goatland. Fiona came with us for the first week, partly to help us with the twins, but Jonathan chose to stay at home. My sister and brother-in-law, Shene and Graham, came to house-sit for us and have a holiday while we were away, so Jonathan had some company. We had a good time, relaxing and visiting Lesley's family who lived nearby. Everyone wanted to see the twins, who were now crawling and into everything.

Coming home rested after the break, I was delighted to see a mountain of mail from colleagues all over the country responding to my Sea Sunday appeal for funds for the new Duddon Inshore Rescue boat. Before going away, I'd spent ages compiling a database and sent out hundreds of emails, and over £3,000 had come in in response. It was worth the hard work. I felt that raising funds, appealing for donations and arranging discounts on equipment was one of the ways in which I could help the work of the lifeboat crew. I was thrilled when, having stepped down from the RNLI chaplaincy, I was asked to become Duddon's chaplain, as well as being an ordinary crew member.

My email database also came in useful when, after four years of interregnum at St Matthews and no sign of a new incumbent on the horizon, I decided to show a bit of initiative and sent out 300 messages to colleagues, appealing for someone to come and work with me in Barrow-in-Furness. There had been no response to the ad that had appeared in the church press the previous year, and the congregation was starting to get despondent at the apparent lack of progress in finding a new rector.

The response to my appeal was overwhelming, with many colleagues contacting me to wish me well, or ask for more details of the position. But not everyone was pleased.

I had a call from the archdeacon.

'Mark, I'm sure you mean well,' he began. 'But I must remind you that it's my job to recruit and appoint to the post of rector. Not yours.'

'I didn't mean to usurp your role, archdeacon,' I apologised. 'I was just frustrated that nothing seems to have happened. And I genuinely thought that a personal appeal from me, pointing out all the positive things about this parish, might help attract the attention of the right person for the job.'

In fact, it took another three years until a new rector was appointed, by which time my relationship with the church hierarchy was virtually at breaking point.

Meanwhile, I carried on, doing my best to show God's love, taking services, visiting my parishoners on the estate, baptising, marrying and burying, and seeking to make the church a welcoming place for everyone. Secretly, I was glad I could escape to the lifeboat station, which was a lifeline for me in many ways.

Lesley was right about my tendency to be over-enthusiastic, though. From the moment I'd joined Duddon Inshore Rescue, I knew I wanted to customise my car. Eventually I went and visited young Wesley at Chatsworth Signs. He loved experimenting and had marked up loads of emergency vehicles, so had a good idea of the sort of thing I wanted. I was delighted when he called to tell me the car was ready.

'What do you think?' I took Lesley by the hand and led her out to the front of the house, where I'd parked the car.

'Oh no! Mark, how could you?' She dropped her head into her hands.

I was disappointed by her reaction.

'Come on, don't you think it's great?' It was a bit bright, I admit, but I thought it looked fabulous. Huge yellow letters ran along the full length of the car, on the bonnet and on the wings. Yellow chequered stripes along the doors, around the back and down the front of the bonnet completed the look. Smaller lettering in the rear window gave my telephone number for donations. Our ordinary family car had been transformed into an emergency vehicle – I even had a bar light on the roof.

Jonathan thought it was great, but Fiona refused to be seen in it – until it started to rain and she did not want her hair to get wet. Lesley came round eventually, although she kept moaning that she could not get the weekly shopping into the boot because it was always full of emergency equipment.

Most of the people on the estate were amused and fully supported my work with Duddon Inshore Rescue. However, there were a few dissenting voices from people within the church who felt I was spending too much time and effort fundraising for Duddon when I should have been concentrating on raising money for the church. In fact, Lesley and I had always tithed our income, giving away ten per cent of all we earned to the church. We rarely claimed our full entitlement of expenses and often gave extra gifts and offerings to parish work.

*

'Vicar, what do you think about bondage?' Was someone playing a prank on me? I'd agreed to take the call from the local newspaper but I did not recognise the voice, so I knew it wasn't Jo, my favourite journalist on the Northwest Evening Mail. I'd worked with Jo a lot and trusted her to write an accurate story. Unlike many of my clergy colleagues, who didn't want to risk being misquoted by the press and gave their local papers a wide berth as a result, I often called the Mail or wrote them a letter about local issues. While some people accused me of being a self publicist – and I have to admit that I am, to a certain extent – I also wanted to give a voice to the many people in my parish who felt under-represented and who felt that their opinions were never sought and their voices never heard. This was something a bit different though – and I immediately realised I needed to be cautious.

'Hmm, that's an interesting question – would you care to elaborate?' I played for time, trying to collect my thoughts.

'Well, the Northwest Bondage Club had booked their AGM and meal at the Owl and Pussycat. Now they've been told that their booking has been withdrawn because there were complaints. People do not like the idea of them being there because it is a family restaurant.'

I did not even know there was a Northwest Bondage Club, but I did not see why they should not have their meal and business meeting wherever they wanted. It is not as though they were going to turn up in fetish gear, complete with whips and chains. If they dressed conventionally, I did not see a problem. But I did not feel it was appropriate to share my thoughts on this occasion: the likely headline if I did – 'Vicar defends bondage' – just would not be helpful!

There were plenty of positive things happening on the estate which I was far happier talking to the press about. Thanks to many good people who were willing to get involved, the community centre was refurbished and became home to Sure Start, working with families and putting on family events. The welfare centre for teenage parents continued to do good work.

Admittedly there were still problems with drugs and occasional outbursts of violence, which hit the headlines from time to time. Once, a drug dealer was set upon by his handlers from Liverpool, who took a machete to him and left him lying in a pool of blood. But PC Ollie's careful intelligence gathering and the support of the majority of the people in the community led to the closing down of most of the drug dens and the imprisonment of the major dealers. I was delighted by the positive outcomes, but to be honest all I'd done myself was support PC Ollie and sit on a number of committees that were committed to tackling crime and antisocial behaviour. I felt the real credit should go to the decent, law-abiding people of the estate. They were the ones who provided the intelligence, had the courage to speak out and actually did something positive to reclaim their streets. During my time in Ormsgill my admiration and respect for them continued to grow.

It is my belief that money does not change a thing. What really works is spiritual transformation: when people change on the inside and begin to value themselves and their friends and neighbours, that's when you can start to see a difference. In my best moments I felt that my presence on the estate, and my regular prayers for the people, were in a small way helping to change the spiritual climate of Ormsgill.

One night I was at home, just contemplating going to bed, when there was a knock on the door. I opened it to see two uniformed police officers, who told me there was an incident on the estate and that the gentlemen involved, who was a bit the worse for drink, would only talk to me.

'Will you come with us, Father Mark?'

'Of course – you go ahead and I'll follow in my own car.'

I knew the young man they referred to well. He had a reputation for being a hard man, and when he'd had a few drinks he'd kick off. I'd been able to build a good relationship with him and the truth was, when he was sober he was a lovely, gentle, calm and rational person. It was the demon drink that brought out the worst in him. Seeing the police arrive would only make him worse, I knew that.

Within minutes I was driving right into what looked like a stand-off between the young man and the police. I could see him in the middle of the road brandishing a heavy iron bar threateningly.

But the minute he saw my car he dropped the bar, ran over and jumped into my passenger seat. I moved off to park on the side of the road. The police surrounded the car as I came to a halt. I wound down the window.

'It's OK, we're fine. Just give us a minute, please, officers.'

The man was really agitated and kept thumping my dashboard with his fists, then banging his head against it. The police watched closely, ready to react at any moment.

All I could do was talk gently to him and give him a hug. Eventually he calmed down enough for me to risk leaving him alone for a moment while I got out of the car.

'What would be the best outcome of this?' I quietly asked the nearest officer, keeping my eye on the man in my car and making sure I didn't make any sudden movements.

'We'd like to take him into custody,' the officer replied. 'He needs to see the duty medical officer. And sober up a bit.'

I slipped back into the car and was able to persuade the man to walk with me over to the police van, where I helped him inside, promising to meet him at the station and stay with him until the doctor came. And I did. It was a long night. I left the police station at 3.30 in the morning, by which time the young man had seen the doctor and was asleep in the cells. I later found out that the incident had been reported on police radio as having been 'contained in the vicar's car'!

On my way back to St Francis house, it occurred to me that they did not teach you this kind of stuff at theological college. In my experience, Christian ministry was an awful lot more than 'more tea, vicar?'!

*

Life in Ormsgill had its colourful moments, but I always enjoyed being out and about on the estate and never felt threatened or afraid, not even walking round at night. I especially loved the summer months, when people sat out on the steps at the front of their houses until late in the evening, or put up deck chairs in the small gardens. The smell of barbeques drifting on the evening air and the sound of kids playing in paddling pools were a real part of summer. During the winter, there would often be friendly snowball fights between neighbours, which I loved to join. PC Ollie was never too happy when the inevitable excited child tried to knock his helmet off with a well-judged snowy missile...

It sounds like a picture of a bygone age, but it really was like that in Ormsgill. There was a neighbourliness and a buzz on the estate that I had not experienced anywhere else.

The post office in the parade of shops was at the heart of the community and I spent a lot of time there, meeting people and generally being visible and accessible. Peter and Linda, the sub-post-master and his wife, had their fingers on the pulse of the community and did a huge amount for it. Fortunately they managed to avoid the post office being closed – in fact, it was refurbished and they asked me to perform a service of blessing in it, sprinkling holy water and praying for the staff and the residents of the Ormsgill estate.

PC Ollie's sub police office was right next door to the post office, and he let me use it to chat with people who needed a bit more privacy. He and I were a good team. But it soon became clear to me that PC Ollie could not police the estate on his own – there was just too much work for one man to do. So I helped the community to run a campaign, writing letters to the paper and to PC Ollie's boss, highlighting all PC Ollie's good work but also highlighting the need for someone to share the load. Eventually it paid off: the Chief Constable promised another community policeman for Ormsgill.

CHAPTER NINE

'This will be the year of the Lord.' I looked at the words I'd just written on the first page of my new journal. I had no idea what they really meant. It was 1st January 2005. Was I making a positive confession of faith, believing and praying that God would soon break through and renew my spirit? Or was I just trying to force myself to face the fact that my crisis of faith was getting worse and I could not seem to find a way out of it? The legacy of my troubled childhood still dogged me and my sudden, uncontrollable outbursts of anger were getting worse. Fiona and Jonathan had started telling me I should go to anger management classes, which made me feel dreadful. I loved my children but I was convinced that I was a failure as a father. I tried to console myself with the fact that most parents struggle with their teenage children. But I knew that was not always the case. Lesley was the perfect mother, not only to the twins but also to the teenagers. I just did not know how to handle my own inner conflict and deal with my children's teenage angst at the same time. I was not proud of how I was feeling and became increasingly frustrated with myself. Thank goodness for the twins, who somehow kept me focused on the importance of family and what it meant to be a father. At least with them I could be the fun-loving dad I longed to be.

'A new year, with endless possibilities,' I wrote. 'The first day of the rest of my life.' I was longing to rediscover my passion for God and my excitement in serving him, but my whole life seemed to revolve round keeping the show on the road and the church afloat, despite all my inner doubts and fears. Not so much 'endless possibilities', more like the pointless repetitions of Groundhog Day.

I was still looking after St Matthews and St Francis, with no sign of a new appointment in sight. Despite my best efforts, the new 11 o'clock service that David had started at St Matthews was failing. I had the idea that if it could be transferred to St Francis, it might suit people on the estate who weren't able to get to the 9 o'clock service. Several families said they'd be interested, and the eight or so people who supported the 11 o'clock service were happy to transfer to St Francis – if the church council agreed. It seemed like the perfect solution.

But nothing in church life is ever simple. After weeks of negotiation and special meetings, I was getting nowhere and feeling worn out.

Things came to a head at yet another church council meeting. The traditionalists could not accept the new service and said it would split the church. I walked out to the kitchen to calm down for a few minutes, before returning to the meeting and declaring that I was throwing in the towel. There would be no new 11 o'clock service at St Francis. I hated feeling that I'd given up, but I could not see a way through.

Fortunately, there were still things to celebrate in the church. St Francis was fifty years old in 2005 and my church wardens had been planning a special celebration weekend for months. Several former clergy came back to take part in a special service, topped off by a garden party at the vicarage. It was all a resounding success – although I did wonder, as I made my speech, whether St Francis would still be around in another fifty years time. I did hope so. Despite everything, I'd grown to love St Francis and the people who worshipped there. The Ormsgill community had pulled together to establish and build the church, paying a pound per brick. It was that sort of spirit that I treasured and hoped would continue, overcoming any pettiness and divisions.

*

'Lesley?'

'Mm?' came the reply from the kitchen.

'Here, look at this.' I walked in and spread the Northwest Evening Mail out over the kitchen table, moving aside the remains of two bowls of fish fingers. The twins were running in and out, shouting incomprehensibly to each other.

Lesley came and hung over my shoulder to see what I was looking at, her hands wet from the washing up.

'Careful! You're dripping on Billie Piper!' I warned.

It was a great picture. There I was, holding a wooden processional cross while dressed as Dr Who, complete with cape, hat and long woolly scarf, superimposed next to Billie Piper, the Doctor's assistant at the time.

'Vicar ready to swap pulpit for Tardis', read the headline.

110

I'd had a bit of fun writing to the BBC saying that I'd like to be considered as a candidate for the next Doctor when Christopher Ecclestone stood down. They replied in the same spirit with a lovely letter saying that regrettably the position had been filled. I must confess I was a little disappointed – sharing the Tardis with Billie Piper was one of my fantasies... The Northwest Evening Mail had taken up the story and arranged the photograph.

'Nice one, hubs,' Lesley gave me a quick hug. 'Very dashing. Boys, come back here. Bath time!'

Not everyone took the picture in the same way, unfortunately. By the time my former church warden, my current church warden and several people from the traditional wing of the church had called me to complain, all my joy over the 50th anniversary celebrations had well and truly disappeared. It had not crossed my mind that anyone would be offended by a picture.

*

'God is dead and the church sucks!' I was clutching the phone so tightly that my knuckles were white. I don't think my friend and colleague Ian Hook was quite expecting such a violent response to his innocent question, 'How are you?'

That was how I felt, though.

To Ian's credit, he did not sound at all shocked.

'Oh, I'm sorry to hear that. Tell me why you feel that way, mate.'

It ended up being a very long phone call, but tell him I did. I needed a listening ear. I did not feel I could talk to Gerald, my spiritual director, as he was grieving the loss of his long term partner and I was trying to support him and cover his services at the hospital. And there was no one else to talk to. That was part of the problem. Apart from a list of counsellors in the clergy handbook, there was simply no procedure in place in the Church of England for dealing with clergy stress and faith issues. I still had two years left to go on my seven year tenure as team vicar, and that was beginning to prey on my mind. The thought of leaving Barrow brought all my insecurities to the fore. But I wondered how much longer I could remain a church minister when my own faith was faltering so much. I felt I was in a difficult position.

'We're meant to care for everyone else,' I concluded, feeling a bit calmer once I'd let off steam. 'But who cares for us?' I couldn't help remembering the case of a popular vicar who'd hung himself in the woods. It made my blood run cold just thinking about it. As well as being a tragedy for the poor man's family, it was a stark reminder of my own suicide attempts. I didn't want to end up like that.

'Look, Mark, come round and chat any time you need to,' Ian said, generously.

'Will do. Thanks. And thanks for listening.'

In the event, I didn't have time to take Ian up on his offer. There was just too much going on.

*

Fiona was nearly eighteen and she and Jonathan were both planning to leave home and go to university. Half the time I was struggling with regret and guilt about not having been a better parent to both of them, and half the time I felt redundant. I hated feeling that my little girl had outgrown me. And I couldn't help worrying about Fiona's future. She'd already had more jobs than I could count and had left each one because she didn't like it. Although I joked with her about the Fiona dolls that I pretended the Northwest Evening Mail were giving away – the ones with a cord to pull to make them say 'I don't like that job. I don't like that job' – I was concerned. She didn't seem able to stick at anything and now she couldn't make up her mind about which university she wanted to go to.

I knocked politely on her bedroom door.

She was lying on the bed poring over a fashion magazine. Clothes were hanging everywhere – she had too many to fit into her wardrobe, but was always complaining she had nothing to wear. I couldn't see the top of her dressing table at all; it was covered in expensive-looking pots of cosmetics, nail varnishes, hair products and jewellery.

'You won't be able to afford all these expensive brands when you're a student,' I said before I could stop myself.

She shrugged her shoulders, with a 'Yeah, Dad, right. Whatever,' sort of look.

I picked my way carefully past one high-heeled sandal and a pair of black patent knee-high boots and sat down on the bed with her.

'I've been thinking, princess.'

Silence.

I soldiered on.

'I know you're finding it difficult to decide what to do next. I was wondering, why do not you do a course at the Further Education College here in Barrow?'

She looked up, her face starting to crumple.

'What's the matter? I think it's a great idea.' I continued, deciding to keep going, although the signs weren't good. I produced my best argument: 'That way you could keep on living at home for a bit longer.'

She flung herself back against her pillows and bawled.

Once again, I'd managed to get on the wrong side of my daughter, the diva. I loved her so much and didn't want to let her go. But I was convinced I was a failure as a parent.

Jonathan was a different kettle of fish entirely. I did not want him to leave home either. He'd finally abandoned his Goth phase and was now constantly fighting Fiona for the hair straighteners. He was into piercings and looked for all the world like an amiable, hairy yeti. He was all set to do a higher national diploma course at Manchester before he began his degree in film and media and sound technology, and was delighted that his long-term girlfriend, Haley, would be going to Manchester too. It would be difficult for Lesley and I financially, with both of the big children leaving home at the same time, but with a bit of belt-tightening and Lesley's skilful financial management, we were determined to make it work.

On a positive note, the twins had settled very well into nursery even though they were still in nappies. The staff were wonderful and it was golden having that time between one and three o'clock when the boys were away - quite frankly Lesley and I needed the break. Picking them up was always a delight and I loved seeing the joy on their faces as they brought us a dripping wet painting or wanted to drag us back into the classroom to see the pet.

Mark Jr continued to have treatment at our local hospital and was admitted on two occasions to Alder Hey children's hospital for a procedure to stretch his oesophagus by having a rubber balloon inserted and blown up. As a result of the surgery he'd had when he was born, apart from having to spend long periods in hospital he also suffered serious reflux. We first became aware of it when he started on solid food and choked every time he tried to eat something. The first procedure he'd had was a success, but as he grew older it had to be repeated several times. Regular visits to the consultant were reassuring for us as his parents, as was our open access to the children's ward. Mark Jr was a very poorly child at times but we just got used to it. The only heart breaking thing was that when he got older he kept asking, 'Mummy why do I have to keep going into hospital? Am I going to die?' There had been many times when we'd asked ourselves the same question, but during those times we had no choice but to pray and rely on God and hope that eventually Mark Jr would be healed.

*

'Come on Mark, you'll be late if you don't hurry up,' shouted Lesley up the stairs.

My best mate Davo had recently got married again, to a lovely woman called Linda. True to form, Davo had chosen to hold the wedding itself in secret, but we'd been invited to the service of blessing in his church in Preston a few weeks later. I was honoured to have been asked to do a reading. And I was so pleased that my friend had found love again.

'Right! I'm ready,' I said, descending the stairs in my clerical suit. Looking rather dapper, I thought.

No sooner had my foot hit the bottom step than my pager went off.

'You can NOT go!' said Lesley, glaring at me.

I checked the screen. 'Immediate launch,' it read. 'Person reported.'

'Les, I've got to go! "Person reported" means that someone's in the water and in trouble.'

Lesley blocked my exit, her arms folded menacingly across her chest.

'Seriously, Les,' I protested, trying to squeeze past. 'Half the crew are at a fundraising event. Look, you go in your car with the twins and I'll be along as soon as I can.'

I could see she was starting to relent.

'Oh, OK then. I'll wait for you,' she conceded. 'We've got time. I suppose. Just don't forget to give me a ring and let me know what's happening. I know you don't want to let Davo down.'

I ran out of the house, attached the roof light to my car, switched on the other emergency lights and drove at speed out of the drive, adrenaline pumping. Cars pulled over and allowed me to pass. In my wing mirror I could see Howard in his Landrover some distance behind, with his emergency lights flashing. 'Good,' I thought. 'At least there are two of us.'

Howard and I arrived at the boat house at the same time as Dave Caldwell. The big blue doors were open and the tractor had already left with the boat and a crew of three.

'We have a report of a male aged about 29, up to his waist in water and cut off by the incoming tide,' reported another crew member.

'Howard, mate, you're driving. Let's get there before the coastguard!' I leapt into Howard's vehicle and we drove off down to the shoreline, sirens on and blue light flashing.

About a half an hour later we were stood down, as reports were coming in that the gentlemen concerned had got himself out of the water and was at home in the bath while the emergency services were out looking for him. He was a jogger who liked to race the tide, despite the obvious dangers to himself and others.

I made Davo's service of blessing with plenty of time to spare.

*

By now, Fiona was almost sure that she would be going to Preston University to study Tourism and Leisure. She'd managed to secure some rather posh student accommodation, complete with en-suite facilities, whereas Jonathan would be sharing with his yeti mates.

Before waving goodbye to our grown-up children, Lesley and I, together with the twins, had the pleasure of attending Kerry's graduation from Preston University. Kerry's personal journey from single mum to honours graduate and, eventually, successful career woman owning her own home, was a true inspiration. She'd come a long way.

She and I were still very close, but not as close as we once were, and I missed it. I longed to share with Kerry how I was feeling about my crisis of faith. But she had been so busy and, with all the demands on my time as well, we just didn't have the chance to chat over coffee at the vicarage any more.

Her life had been completely turned around when she found God, and her faith was now a lot stronger than mine. Her involvement with her church had grown and grown and "Hyper Holly" went along to all the young people's events. Holly was a credit to Kerry and had a smile to melt your heart. Not that it worked on her mother, who did not hesitate to discipline Holly when she needed it. I still baby-sat for Holly sometimes while Kerry went out with her new young man. Was I jealous? Well, yes and no. I had Lesley: she was my wife and I would always be faithful to her and to my marriage vows, but that didn't stop me being a bit jealous because Kerry now spent more time with her boyfriend than she did with me. On the other hand, I was very happy for her.

Kerry gave me the biggest hug after the graduation ceremony was over and for a moment we just held each other.

'Thanks, Mark, for all your support over the years. I couldn't have done it without you,' she said.

'I love you Kerry, I always will, you know that. I'm so pleased for you, and I'm proud to call you my friend.' I took a step back. 'You look great in your cap and gown!'

She hugged me tighter and whispered in my ear, 'I love you too, Mark. You're the best friend ever.'

Lesley was waiting to add her congratulations. Kerry released me and flung her arms round my wife.

When Kerry had been whisked away by her aunties and friends, Lesley and I looked at each other.

'Just think,' said Lesley. 'In a few years' time we'll be doing this with Jonathan and Fiona.'

'I know. It's a sobering thought, isn't? It will not be long before they've left the nest for the big wide world,' I agreed, rather gloomily.

And sure enough, the day I did not want to arrive soon did. Fiona spent hours and hours packing boxes and worrying about whether she'd be able to fit everything in. Jonathan did not seem to have much to pack at all – and he was far more laid back about the whole process anyway. We'd arranged to split Fiona's things between the two cars: Fiona herself would travel with me and the twins with Lesley. Jonathan was happy to be picked up by the father of a mate of his.

Suddenly, everything was ready and it was time to go.

I stood facing Jonathan. His hair virtually obscured his face; he was a good looking lad underneath it all, but it was hard to tell.

'Goodbye, son,' I said, hugging him tightly. He hugged me back.

'Love you, Dad,' he said.

'Love you too, son.' I could feel the tears start to prick my eyes.

'Cheer up, Dad, I'll be back at Christmas!'

We hugged again, then I had to walk away.

Fiona demanded my attention

'Dad, I'm not going without that pink suitcase! It's got all my hair products in it.'

'Sweetheart, it's already in the boot.'

And so we set off for Preston. From the moment we touched base, Fiona was in a world of her own, as her friends arrived and they greeted each other with giggles and screams of excitement. The twins wandered up and down the halls of residence, getting into everything, and insisting on undoing Fiona's cases and emptying the contents on the floor. Lesley tried to distract them while I was the work horse, loading things into the lift for Fiona to unload at the top. It took 45 minutes to get sorted out, then it was time to say goodbye.

I was subdued all the way home, with memories of my kids' childhoods filling my thoughts. Memories of the fights and squabbles over the last few years as they and I struggled to adjust to the teenage years. Memories of Lesley constantly acting as peacemaker. And the happy memories - family occasions, family holidays, birthdays and Christmases. How quickly children grow up.

When we got back, Lesley and I both went into Jonathan's room and sat on his bed. The room was empty, but still managed to look untidy, even without him in it. I couldn't hold my emotions in any longer, and cried and cried into my son's pillow until I was exhausted. When I sat up, I could hear Lesley putting the twins to bed in the next room. I looked round at Jonathan's bare walls and thought what a horrible colour dark green was. I'd redecorate before he came home at Christmas.

*

There's nothing quite like another birthday to remind you of the passing years. I must admit I fail to see what's so wonderful about the ageing process, but I do like the presents – and I always pretend that I'm a year younger than I am, which amuses my friends and makes me feel slightly better.

'Happy birthday, darling,' announced Lesley, walking into the bedroom with the twins in close attendance, their arms full of presents. Mark and Joshua jumped onto the bed and bounced up and down on me.

'Happy birthday dada!' they chorused.

I grabbed them by the legs and tickled them mercilessly.

'Come on boys,' Lesley reminded them. 'Give Daddy his presents.'

Joshua and Mark started tearing the paper off the chocolate that they'd wrapped up for me. They wanted to 'help' me eat it straight away and Lesley had to wrestle it away from them, promising they could have some later. Once there was no more paper to tear off, they lost interest and went back to their own bedroom to play. It was strange, following the family tradition of opening my birthday presents in bed without Jonathan and Fiona being there too.

Lesley perched on the side of the bed and looked at me.

'What's up? Don't you like your presents?'

'Oh no, it's not that - they're great! I'm just a bit fed up. I miss Jonathan and Fiona, and I can't stop wondering where my life is going.'

Lesley sidled closer to me and stroked my head.

'Why do you still love me?' I mumbled, feeling that I was letting her down again. 'I know I haven't been easy to live with lately. I'm grumpy, I fly off the handle at the slightest thing, I don't feel motivated by church life, I'm tired and depressed. And I feel so empty inside.'

She slid a warm hand under my stubbly chin and looked straight into my eyes. 'I love you, Mark, because you've got so many good qualities. Sometimes I feel helpless when you shut us all out and retreat into yourself, but I'm praying for you. I'm praying that God will break through and re-energize you.'

'You're too good for me,' I would happily have drowned in her eyes. 'I don't like myself very much at the moment. I feel I've failed Jonathan and Fiona, I've made so many mistakes as a parent.'

Lesley put both arms round me. 'Of course you have. Everyone does. But you're wonderful with the twins and they adore you.'

I could not stop being hard on myself. 'But what about Fiona and Jonathan? Do they hate me?'

'No, silly, of course they don't! You've got to learn to forgive yourself, Mark.'

'It's not that easy,' I said into her shoulder. 'I feel as though I'm living a lie. I put on that dog collar, I perform my duties, I pastor my flock, I pray for the sick, I support the bereaved, counsel the vulnerable, hold the hand of the dying, look after two parishes and keep the show on the road. But God seems so distant.'

'Mark, I still believe in you. You're a great priest. I know how hard you've fought to get to where you are today and I know you're not a quitter. God will show up, I know he will. Just hold on. Just give him time.'

Right on cue, we were interrupted by loud bangings coming from the twins' bedroom.

'No peace for the wicked,' remarked Lesley, getting up off the bed. 'Your other present will have to wait.'

'What other present?' I asked excitedly.

'Birthday spanks!' she said with a grin, dodging the pillow I threw at her retreating figure.

'By the way,' I said, just as she reached the door. 'I've bought you something too.'

'Oh? What?'

'A skirt.'

'What sort of skirt?'

'Short. Very short.'

'Mark! What are you like? Are you trying to get me into trouble?'

'You'll be fine so long as you don't wear it to church. I don't think the verger would approve.'

'Never mind the verger, I don't think my mother would approve!'

'Well, I didn't buy it for your mother, did I?'

Lesley laughed and chucked the pillow back at me.

*

In fact, although Fiona had physically left home, there were days when it didn't seem like it. She texted and called us all the time, wanting me to sort out everything from her TV to her project work. It was as though her mobile was an umbilical cord, keeping her attached to the security of home. It wasn't as though she was unhappy – she'd thrown herself into university life, and had got a job she loved, working in the student club, "55 degrees". She burned the candle at both ends and then complained about feeling stressed. I did wonder how my dear daughter would manage to get through the next three years.

As ever, Jonathan was the exact opposite. We had to call him from time to time to just to check that he was still alive. I had not forgotten my plan to redecorate his room but I was not prepared for the hidden horrors that awaited me. Empty crisp and sweet packets had been shoved down behind the bed and empty cans of lager abandoned in corners. White, fuzzy patches of mould grew on the remains of left-over food and there were drips of candle wax all over the carpet. Worst of all, when we moved the bed we discovered the entire contents of a bottle of spilt milk. It took days and a lot of disinfectant to get rid of the sour curdled smell.

I laughed and cried in turns as I set to and transformed Jonathan's room. I missed him so much. Mind you, I had to be vigilant, because the twins were keen to join in with the painting. Once they sneaked in while I was up a ladder and helped themselves to a couple of brushes. They'd started 'redecorating' Fiona's room before I realised they'd gone suspiciously quiet and gone to look for them. It's amazing how much mess two determined three-year-olds can make. 'At least having the two of them around helps to fill the hole left by Jonathan and Fiona's departures,' I thought, scrubbing the paint off them as they giggled and splashed in the bath.

CHAPTER TEN

'Bless these little boys,' I said to Lesley as I dragged the box of Pampers out of the car boot. 'When will they be out of nappies?' We'd had some success, and Joshua more than Mark had responded positively to sweets as a reward for a deposit in the potty, but when we tried them in pants there were accidents and a whole lot of mess to clean up. It was like following a couple of little dogs around with a poop scooper. And I'll never forget the night that Fiona helped bath them and the screams that followed as they decided to do a poo in the bath on her watch.

I could hear Mark Jr and Joshua shrieking happily as they raced round my brother-in-law's house, discovering their cousins' toys and generally causing mayhem. Lesley and I were having a holiday in her home town of Selby this year, and were using my brother-in-law's house while he and his family were away.

I carried the cases up to the master bedroom, took off my shoes and wriggled my toes into the deep pile carpet. It was lovely to experience a bit of luxury. I threw myself onto the bed and lay back on the squishy pillows with my hands behind my head, closing my eyes with a contented sigh.

My thoughts drifted back to the service I'd taken at St Francis the previous evening. For the past few years I'd combined the celebration of St Francis tide with All Souls Eve into one service. Everyone who had been bereaved during the previous year was invited to come and light a candle to remember their loved ones. Although there were some people who did not like it, the combination of the two services virtually guaranteed a full church and this year was no exception.

Gerald Garbutte, my friend and spiritual director, was the regular guest speaker at the service. This year was his last time, as he was due to retire. I think he was quite relieved – it was not easy having to find a sermon subject which fitted St Francis tide *and* All Souls Eve *and* the sensitivities of the recently bereaved, year after year.

As I lay comfortably on the bed, unwinding from the journey to Selby, I suddenly found myself laughing uncontrollably. The bed wobbled underneath me and I started to choke. I pushed myself to a sitting position, thinking I was about to have an asthma attack, but great waves of laughter kept rolling over me.

'Whatever's the matter with you?' asked Lesley, as she came in with one of the smaller suitcases.

'Last night's service.' I spluttered, tears streaming down my cheeks.

'What about it?' Lesley put the case down and jumped onto the bed beside me. The resulting bounce made me giggle some more. I drew a deep breath and tried not to look at her.

'Gerald,' I snorted.

Lesley thumped me on the shoulder.

'Stop it! Tell me properly.'

'Well, you know that I've got a new server? He's still learning how to perform some of the rituals for the high services. Anyway, I incensed the altar and handed the censer to him so that he could incense the rest of the church. He bowed so low as he walked off between the pews swinging the censer that he looked like Quasimodo! And Gerald whispered to me … he whispered,' - I could feel a new wave of laughter rising in my chest – 'Gerald said, "He looks as though he's looking for mice. Does he work for Rentokil?"'

I rolled over and buried my face in the pillow to muffle my guffaws.

'By the time he'd finished with the incense I could hardly see him, there was so much smoke in the church. Everyone was coughing and two women had to go out to get some fresh air.'

The server was a lovely man, generous and committed and enthusiastic. I'd told him after the service what Gerald had said and he'd laughed and commented that mice or no mice, at least the church had been well incensed.

Lesley chuckled and smacked me across the bottom as she got up.

'Very funny. Never mind that now, come and help me with the boys. We need to do the food shopping before we go and see Mum and Dad and my sister.'

I rolled over and threw the pillow at her, narrowly missing her as she slipped out of the door. It was good to get away and laugh and relax.

By the evening, however, Lesley and I were both exhausted. The twins had had fun at the in-laws' house, grabbing everything in sight, particularly the things they were not supposed to touch. The dried flowers would have to be replaced but fortunately I'd managed to stick out my hand and catch the glass vase before it hit the fire surround. We did not stay long at Lesley's sister Alison's either.

At last, the boys were safely tucked up in bed and asleep, looking angelic. Mark Jr was clutching one of his cousin's dolls. He did not care that boys were not meant to play with dolls, he just loved new toys. I kissed them both on their warm, smooth foreheads, told them I loved them and went downstairs to chill out on the settee in front of the television.

I was idly channel-hopping when Lesley appeared, dressed for bed, with a cup of coffee for me. I sat up and took the mug.

'Thanks, sweetheart. Any news from Fiona or Jonathan?'

Lesley settled down beside me, tucking her legs underneath her.

'Fiona texted me this morning saying she was stressed out, but there's been nothing from Jonathan. You know what he's like – we'll hear soon enough when he's short of money!'

If truth be told, I hardly ever worried about Jonnie. He'd been independent for a long time, even before he left home to go to college. His long term relationship with Haley continued to flourish, despite opposition from her foster mum. It was nice that Jonathan and Haley were able to go to Manchester and study together. Sooner or later they'd have to knuckle down to work, but for now they were immersed in the student sub-culture of partying and drinking as much as possible. It had always surprised me how readily both Jonathan and Fiona had got drawn into binge drinking. Alcohol had never been part of our life at home. Lesley had stopped drinking when she met me, as she didn't want to be a stumbling block and I'd vowed never to touch alcohol after it played a major part in my breakdown and suicide attempts. I'm proud to this day that our wedding was alcohol free and everyone still had a great time.

'Penny for your thoughts?' asked Lesley.

'Oh, nothing. I was just thinking about the kids. I do worry about Fiona. She's such a drama queen. How many times has she texted or phoned since she left for Preston? She's already been home for two weekends, complaining about being stressed out, and she hasn't even started her first assignment yet.'

'You do love a good worry, don't you?' Lesley hit the nail on the head, as usual.

'Hmm, yes, I suppose so. It's nice to know that my little muppet still needs her daddy. Although I could do without her passing all her stresses on to me!'

'What are you going to be like when your little princess gets a boyfriend?'

'Don't say that! Any boy who comes near Fiona will have to get past me first!' I shuddered, remembering the spotty herberts who'd hung around her at sixth form college. I'd told one lad, who arrived at our house with a crash helmet and a sheepish expression, that if he went up to Fiona's bedroom with her he had to keep both his feet on the floor when he sat on the bed. And I'd gone up and knocked on her door several times to make sure that he was obeying the rules. My daughter was beautiful and boys were like bees round a honeypot with her.

Lesley laughed. 'I'm going up to bed,' she said, yawning and stretching. She stood up. 'Are you going to be OK? I know you've had a hard week and a long day.'

'I'll be fine. I'll just vegetate here for a bit and try and find something decent to watch.'

I kept the TV on but turned the sound down. Night-time stillness crept over the house and I was alone with my thoughts. I was glad of the chance to escape, to relax and spend time with Lesley and the twins. It was a miracle that we were here at all. But deep inside, I was afraid. It was such a long time since I'd felt close to God. I still believed in him, but the passion had gone and I didn't know how to get it back. The really terrifying thought was that my whole life depended on my faith. If I was losing it, how could I continue to be a priest? And if I was no longer a priest, what would I do? How would I provide for my family?

My pocket Gideon New Testament sat on the coffee table beside my head as I lay slouched on the settee. With a heavy heart I sat up and opened it at the beginning. The heading, 'Far from God' caught my eye. That was me, no question. I turned to the passage it suggested, James chapter 4, verse 8, and read it slowly: 'Come near to God and he will come near to you.'

If only it were that easy. I'd tried so many times to come near to God through the daily offices of prayer and each time it felt dry and formal. I was frustrated and lonely.

A big, despairing sigh welled up from inside me. I honestly didn't know what to do. But I knew I had to do something. There was nowhere else for me to turn, so I closed my eyes and, for the first time in ages, I prayed a real, personal prayer which came straight from my heart, not from a book.

'Father, I hear what you say through your servant James. I just want you to know that I do not like being the way I am. I long to know you again as I once did. If you're listening, I turn to you in Jesus' name and ask that you refresh and revitalise my weak faith. I'm so sorry that I've failed you and the people I love. Thank you for hearing my prayer. Amen.'

I do not know if I expected anything to happen, but nothing did. I didn't feel a sense of God's presence. My heart didn't beat any faster. If anything, I felt nervy and slightly embarrassed, almost as if I'd been caught out doing something I shouldn't have been doing.

I swung my legs back onto the settee, picked up the remote, turned up the sound and began channel hopping. Flipping quickly past the adult movies, I ended up on the God Channel. A loud-mouthed Texan was jumping up and down, shouting about faith and prosperity and confessing scripture.

'Faith comes by hearing and hearing by the word of God,' he said. 'Put the Word first and your faith will grow! Prosperity isn't about money, it's about the blessing of God on our lives. Abraham's blessing is ours by faith. We're the heirs of the promise through Christ, and that includes your finances. No word in, no faith out! If you believe, faith works. If you don't, then it doesn't. It's not my job to convince you. Good night and God bless!'

With that, he was gone. I was not impressed. 'Loud mouthed Yank,' I thought, 'What do you know?' Everything he said meant that he'd be labelled a fanatic and drummed out of any theological college I'd ever come across. All my theological training screamed 'heresy!'

I'd had enough. I switched off the TV and sat for a moment, wondering why a fanatic like this was even given air time. I turned out the light and went upstairs to bed, feeling rather agitated.

But I could not get to sleep. Tossing and turning, I kept mulling over what the preacher had said. His words seemed to echo in my mind, speaking deep inside my heart. My spirit, like that of John Wesley, the founder of Methodism, was strangely warmed. The more I thought, the more excited I became, but I could not work out why. Finally, a sense of peace washed over me, my body and mind relaxed and I went to sleep, determined to find out more about the man and his teaching.

*

Next day, Lesley kept asking me if I was OK. I still felt inexplicably peaceful but I was not ready to talk to her yet.

'Oh, I'm fine. It's just good to get away and let everything go for a while. Let's try and have a good day!'

And we did. The twins loved the railway museum and the castle museum in York. It did my heart good to see them racing about, chatting and laughing. York Castle is a special place for me – I visited it for the first time on a school trip when I was living in the children's home in Spalding. I could not afford the entrance fee, so my form teacher, Mr Matthews, paid for me. Every time I visit York and see the castle on the hill, I think of Mr Matthews and his kindness. But now, lovely though the day was, I could not wait until the boys and Lesley were in bed.

At last, the twins were settled upstairs, after their usual bedtime routine of baths, stories, tickles, prayers and general mayhem. Lesley and I cuddled up on the settee, breathing sighs of relief. As usual, her twitchy leg syndrome soon got the better of her, as well as annoying the hell out of me. She pulled my head down until it was resting on her chest.

'Let's go to bed, Mark.'

'Hmm, not yet, I think I'll stay here and watch a bit of TV.' Tonight I had something on my mind, and for once it wasn't sex.

The minute Lesley had gone upstairs I grabbed the remote and switched on. I scrolled eagerly through the God channels, one by one. All day I'd felt different, as though something spiritual was stirring inside me. Despite my initial suspicion, all I could think was, I need to hear more of this teaching. Had God answered my heartfelt prayer? I was beginning to dare to believe that he had – but now I needed to listen to that preacher again.

'Father, please help me to find him,' I prayed, my thumb pressing frantically on the remote.

And there he was.

'Welcome to the Believers' Voice of Victory,' his confident voice boomed out. 'Faith comes by hearing and hearing by the word of God! Have you got your ears open, partners? Good, because I have a word from God just for you. Stay tuned!'

For the next half hour I listened, entranced, as Kenneth Copeland bounced all over the stage, preaching with a passion, authority and enthusiasm the like of which I'd never seen before. I hung on his every word, my own spirit leaping for joy in response to what I was hearing, like an excitable child discovering a new bug under a rock.

Every night for the rest of our holiday, as soon as the house was quiet I tuned in to Kenneth Copeland and the BVOV broadcast. I later discovered that this man was part of the Faith Movement and he had many critics, but for now I didn't care. His ministry had done what all my religion and theology and ritual hadn't done. He'd re-awakened me to God and I felt as excited as if I was falling in love for the first time. God had heard my prayer and answered it in a way I could never have expected.

*

'Mark?' Lesley walked into my study, about six weeks after we'd got home from holiday, and plonked herself down on the settee.

'Yes, love of my life?'

'Can we talk?' She looked serious.

'Sure. What's on your mind?'

'You!'

'Why? What have I done now?'

'Don't look so guilty! You haven't done anything. For once!' she smiled, her brown eyes crinkling at the corners. Then she looked away and a tiny shadow flitted across her face. 'But you are different,' she continued. 'What's happened to you?'

I put one finger under her chin and tilted her face gently up towards mine. As I looked at her and read the concern and worry in her expression, I thought how blessed I was to have this beautiful girl as my wife. God had brought us together and she had stuck with me through thick and thin. She was always forgiving, always calm, always loving, even when I was in the depths of despair and felt that everything around me was falling apart.

'Different how?' I asked.

'Well, you haven't had a single outburst of anger for ages, for one thing. And when you preach, you sound so enthusiastic! You're reading the Bible and praying more than you ever used to and you're even talking differently. What's going on?' Her eyes held mine.

For the next twenty minutes I talked and talked, telling Lesley how I'd rediscovered God through the ministry of a brash Texan preacher called Kenneth Copeland. I could feel faith and excitement rising up inside me as I spoke, making my heart beat faster and bringing warmth to my body.

'Wow, Mark! What can I say?' Lesley's eyes were wide but I knew she had an analytical mind and a cool head on her shoulders and was never one to be overcome by emotion. 'I can't deny that I've seen changes for the better in you,' she continued. 'It thrills me to hear you talking about God so positively and getting so excited about faith and reading the Bible. But really, some of the things you've just come out with…!'

'What do you mean?'

'Well, they're a bit wacky. Fanatical...'

'Praise God for that, I'll take that as a compliment,' I exclaimed. 'Do you think anyone else has noticed?'

'If they haven't yet, they soon will. I know what you're like with a new idea. You can be a bit obsessive at times. Remember what you did to the car when you first joined Duddon Inshore Rescue? You've got so many emergency lights on it now it lights up like a Christmas tree whenever you get a call out! And I still can't get the shopping in the boot because of all the rescue gear.' She laughed and drew away. She started fiddling with the corner of one of the cushions and I had a feeling I knew what was coming next.

'Mark, I'm delighted. Really I am. It's a real answer to my prayers that you've rediscovered God. But let me ask you – you've not tapped into some sort of cult, have you? Are you sure you're not being brainwashed?'

I jumped onto the settee with her and squeezed her in my arms. 'No, I haven't joined a cult. But I am being brainwashed – brainwashed by the word of God. I'm just doing what the Bible teaches, I'm allowing God's word to renew my mind and my thinking and my speaking. Ken Copeland's teaching is about confessing scripture: taking God at his word and making positive confessions, speaking out what he has already said in the Bible. Honestly, Les, I've been a Christian for more than twenty years, and I've been to theological college, but I've never heard anything like this before.'

'That's amazing. I must admit I'm a bit jealous. My faith has got dry too. I've been praying for ages that God'll do something new in my own life.'

Lesley's revelation surprised me. She always seemed such a faithful believer - quietly praying, trusting and getting on with things. I suppose I'd become so absorbed in my own struggles that I had not noticed hers. It would not be the first time in our relationship that I'd made that mistake.

I kissed her on the nose.

'Sweetheart, I had no idea.'

'I love you, Mark.'

We sat on the settee for a while, holding each other close. Lesley told me she wanted to hear some of Kenneth Copeland's teaching for herself. She was still concerned about what I might have got myself into, but she couldn't ignore the changes in me.

'The boys are quiet,' I said after a while.

'Hmm, yes. Always a worrying sign. I'd better go and see what they're up to.' She tried to get up, but I hung on to her, stroking her hair and kissing her forehead. She didn't resist but closed her eyes, like she always did when we kissed, and she started to kiss me back. I felt so close to her at that moment – and I was getting turned on.

We were rudely interrupted by a loud knock at the study window.

'Who's that?' I couldn't see, as the blinds were half drawn. I pushed Lesley away and had a discreet peek out of the window.

'Blooming heck, his timing is irritating!'

'Whose?' Lesley said, tucking her blouse back into her jeans.

'Constable Ollie!' I exclaimed. 'I'd better go and let him in. You know what he's like. He'll have seen both cars in the drive so he knows we're both here.'

'I'll go and put the kettle on,' smiled Lesley as she made for the door.

Constable Ollie did not look in the best of moods as I let him in.

'What's up, Ollie?'

'Bloody inspector!' he fumed.

'What's going on? Tell me all about it,' I said, ushering him into the study. 'Lesley's organising tea – and before you ask, there are biscuits.'

PC Ollie strode over to the settee. 'These cushions look a bit dishevelled,' he commented, lowering himself down carefully. 'What have you been doing – jumping on them?'

I laughed. Good old Ollie.

'Not exactly,' I said.

*

Over the next few months I felt like I'd fallen in love with God all over again.

I was excited about life and about ministry in a way that I hadn't been for a long time. Suddenly the Bible started to speak to me again as I spent more time reading it and praying, not out of a sense of duty, but because I wanted to. I no longer felt that I was just going through the motions. My spirit had come alive to God again and it was the most exciting thing imaginable.

Lesley loved the new me and was filled with real optimism for the future. I couldn't stop sharing my new-found spirituality and my very real sense of having discovered something about faith and God that had eluded me all these years.

Many of my colleagues were clearly worried that I was off again on one of my obsessive fads. The rural dean warned that I might come back down to earth with a bump. He told me not to get too carried away with Ken Copeland's teaching, which was considered to be heretical and theologically suspect. To be honest, I was disappointed by the reactions I was getting. I'd naively expected my fellow priests to share my joy. Even my friend Ian Hook kept giving me concerned looks, although he was delighted with my enthusiasm for God. Davo, as always, was objective. He felt that anything that got me back into God could not be a bad thing. But he also knew me well enough to realise that I could get carried away by new things and end up falling flat on my face once the novelty had worn off. However, when he saw that Lesley was also embracing this new teaching he remained open-minded and non-judgmental.

Not everyone at St Francis appreciated the changes, as my teaching became more faith-orientated and challenging. One of my church wardens eventually found my services irritating rather than inspirational and decided to leave, taking his wife with him to a more traditional church. He left with a tear in his eye and I missed him. Despite our differences, he had been a good church warden and I respected him, even though I suspect he simply tolerated me.

It is hard to describe the impact that Ken Copeland's ministry was beginning to have on my life. The more I listened to his teaching, the more I realised that my faith had been impoverished because I didn't understand the principles and laws that applied to developing it.

I could not get enough of this new (to me) way of approaching faith. As the weeks went by, not a day passed without another package of tapes, CDs or DVDs arriving from the KCM office. I listened to Ken Copeland in the car; when I had my morning shower he was on the shower CD player. I even went to sleep listening to him. I was feeding my spirit with the word of God day and night, and it was beginning to have a huge impact on my life. Within a very short time my ministry was renewed, my marriage was renewed, and my relationships with people I'd had problems with before were beginning to change. Usually it was not the other person who had altered, it was me and my reaction to them.

Anger and strife had started to become things of the past. I was now very much aware that if anything was going to hinder my walk with God, it was strife. It had to be cut out of my life. The New Testament was very clear about that. Why I hadn't seen it before, I don't know. Maybe, like many Christians, I'd been selective when it came to applying Bible teaching. It's all too easy to dismiss the passages which make us uncomfortable or which challenge us to actually live like Christians.

I could not wait to share with Kerry what had been happening in my life over the last few months. We finally arranged to meet at her house. She sat perched on the end of her settee, listening carefully as I enthusiastically talked about how much I'd been struggling and how I'd recently rediscovered my faith through an unexpected encounter with a brash American preacher. I thought she'd be absolutely delighted, but as I drew my story to a close I wasn't getting good signals from her. She looked more and more serious.

'Well Kerry, what do you think?' I concluded, smiling hopefully at up her.

She swept her hair back off her face in an impatient gesture then got up and walked towards the French doors. She stood looking out at the garden.

'Aren't you pleased that I've re-discovered God?' I looked at her upright back and tried to keep a pleading note out of my voice.

She whipped round and glared at me.

'No! I'm bloody angry with you!'

Uh-oh.

'Why? I don't understand!' I could feel my palms getting sweaty. This wasn't the reaction I'd been expecting.

'You and I are supposed to be friends and all this time you were hiding behind that bloody collar again, pretending that you were OK! I thought you and I had an understanding.'

'It's not like that, Kerry…'

'Don't interrupt! I'm so disappointed that you've kept all this from me. I love you, Mark. You're my dearest friend. If it wasn't for you I would never have found God. I wouldn't ever have managed to get through all my studying. You and Lesley and the twins are very special to me and you promised me that you wouldn't hide behind that damn collar anymore.' There was a tiny wobble in her voice as she finished, although her face was like thunder.

'Kerry, I love you too, you know that. Lesley and the twins and I adore you and Hyper Holly. I wasn't trying to deceive you, honestly. It's just that I felt so ashamed.' I could hear a tremor in my voice now. 'I was too embarrassed to admit that I was struggling. I thought that if you knew it might affect your faith, just at a time when you were growing so much as a Christian yourself.'

Kerry stood there for a minute, head down, her hair covering her face. Then she looked up. Her expression softened. She sat back down beside me and gave me a huge hug.

'Oh, Mark, I do love you, you silly little man.'

I squeezed her tight.

'I'm sorry, Kerry. I should have shared with you, but you've been busy too. And I guess it's still hard for me sometimes to step outside the role of priest, even with you.'

'Well let's do something about that' she said, grabbing my dog-collar and yanking it out of my shirt. Before I realised what was going on, she'd disappeared into the kitchen with it.

'Kerry? What are you doing?'

She returned brandishing a pair of scissors. I tried to grab the collar off her but she was too quick for me and with one snip, there it was in two pieces.

I could not help laughing. It was partly with relief that our friendship seemed to be restored, even though my collar was ruined.

*

I started 2006 with much optimism and hope for the future. Everything was so different from the same time the previous year. Back then I was almost ready to throw in the towel, give up the priesthood and try to build a life outside the church. Now I felt that anything was possible.

It was lovely to have Fiona, Johnnie and Haley around for Christmas. Johnnie could not believe the transformation of his bedroom and asked why it couldn't have been like that while he was at home? I did point out that it was him who'd chosen the dark green paint and preferred to decorate the room with unwashed clothes, empty crisp packets, dripping candles and his very own DIY air-freshener of a bottle of spilt milk…

It did not take long for both Fiona and Jonathan to notice the difference in me. Lesley sat them down and explained that for a long time I'd been hiding a crisis of faith, but that I'd recently had a spiritual re-awakening. The children were thrilled, and very forgiving of my past flaws. I had a few deep conversations with Johnnie in particular and apologised to him for not always getting it right as a parent. I was very conscious of all the times we'd argued.

'I feel I've let you down, mate,' I said.

'Aw, come on Dad! Don't beat yourself up.' He gave me a man-hug. I still couldn't get used to how tall he was. 'You're a good Pop.'

His generosity brought a lump to my throat.

Mark Jr was rushed into hospital again just before Christmas, but he was out by Boxing Day, so we exchanged our presents then. My gift from Lesley was a lovely new leather-bound Bible. Inside she'd written:

'Dear Mark, only God could do what he has been doing in your life over the last three months. Keep giving him first place in your life. He has given you back your life, your marriage, your family and your ministry. Praise him. Isn't it exciting seeing what God is doing? Let's move forward into 2006 letting the word of life live in us. Love, Lesley xx.'

She'd summed up the last few months exactly. I reached over the piles of mangled wrapping paper and happy children and grabbed hold of her to kiss her, much to the disgust of the older kids, who felt we were too old for such shenanigans. Fiona was particularly offended by the sexy outfits I'd bought for Lesley.

'You two are disgusting,' she said, with a curl of the lip. 'And as for those hooker boots – yuck!' Just as well I'd hidden the rubber skirt I was intending to give Lesley later on.

CHAPER ELEVEN

It was not long before my new-found faith and optimism were to be severely tested. I was sound asleep on the night of January 21 when the ringing of the telephone woke me up. Lesley was working nights, so I reached across her empty side of the bed and answered it.

'Dad? It's me, Johnnie.'

I sat up, suddenly wide awake. My son's voice sounded odd. Something was wrong.

'What's up, son?'

'It's Haley. She's dying.'

'What do you mean? Where are you?'

'At the hospital. Dad, she's been in an accident. They're operating on her now.'

I could feel the tears starting to fill my eyes as Johnnie told me that Haley had been crossing the road outside a nightclub in Manchester when she'd been struck by a car travelling at 80 mph. She'd gone flying up into the air but the driver hadn't stopped. Her injuries were terrible and she wasn't expected to survive.

All I could do was pray, 'Lord, what can I say to my son?' As soon as the question formed in my mind, I heard a voice in my spirit respond, 'Tell him that by my stripes she will be healed. She won't die if you believe.'

I recognised the reference to Isaiah chapter 55, from the Old Testament.

'Son,' I said, 'this might sound strange to you, but I believe God has just spoken to me and said by his stripes she will be healed. Can you believe that?'

'Dad, my faith isn't as strong as yours. But I've just been reading my New Testament here in the hospital chapel. I will believe.'

'OK, son, have faith. Phone me again in the morning. I love you.'

'I love you too, Dad.'

I put the phone down and immediately fear tried to enter my spirit. I knew that fear was the opposite of faith and that fear tolerated was faith contaminated. Now I had to put this teaching to the test. Would I give into fear and depression or would I stand on what I believed and speak words of life over Haley? I did the latter.

I prayed a simple prayer of healing for her, went back to bed and slept peacefully for the rest of the night.

Still, the news was a shock to the whole family and something we had to come to terms with. Fiona kept saying, 'What if Haley dies?' Lesley and I corrected her and told her to stop speaking words of death and believe for Haley's healing, as we were.

When Jonathan phoned again he told us that Haley was still alive but the consultant had said she was going to lose a leg.

'No she won't, son,' I told him. 'Your mum and I will pray against that. And KCM have put Haley on their international prayer list.'

As time went on, for every negative report we got from the hospital, we prayed the opposite. It was not easy, because we were still learning how to put our faith to work. And nothing could take away the human emotions we all felt. We cried a lot but continued to stand on our faith for Haley and Jonathan. We were also careful about what we said out loud, making sure that we did not make any negative confessions as far as Haley was concerned.

Over the next few months, Jonathan kept vigil at Haley's bedside, his studies taking second place to his sense of devotion to the girl he had loved for all these years. She didn't lose a leg but remained in an induced coma for eight weeks. Jonathan was told that she would probably be in a vegetative state because of brain damage. Again we prayed against that report.

Haley eventually came out of the coma and began the long journey to recovery.

I was so proud of Jonathan. He kept a calm head on his shoulders, and for a young lad the stoicism and maturity he showed were far beyond his years. He visited Haley daily for two years, helping with her physio, feeding her, dressing her and taking care of all her needs. When she eventually came out of hospital, he moved in to look after her in specially adapted accommodation, in effect becoming her full time carer.

Sadly, after three years Jonathan felt that the relationship had come to an end and he and Haley parted company. It was a painful time for both of them. Haley was able to return to University, but after trying to restart his course Jonathan decided to postpone it indefinitely. It was the right decision; emotionally the lad was a wreck and he needed time to work out his pain and his anger. He eventually moved into a rented house in Manchester with some of his yettie friends from Barrow and began working full time with disabled people, a career which suited his caring nature.

*

'Mark, listen to this,' giggled Lesley as she sat in the kitchen reading the local paper. '"Dear vicar, come up and see us some time, when we've got nothing on."'

'Oh boy. Tell me you're kidding,' I grabbed the Evening Mail from her.

She was not. Underneath the headline, two scantily-clad girls leant forward seductively. Further inspection revealed that the column was a response to my protest over the proposed plan to open a lap dancing club in Barrow. The owners were asking if I wanted to get up close and personal with the dancers, in a bid to make me change my mind.

'So - are you going?' asked Lesley

'What do you think?' I raised my eyebrows and tried to look stern.

'I think that part of you would love to,' she teased.

'Funny girl. I'm sure the bishop would have something to say if I set foot inside a lap dancing club.'

Lesley laughed. 'Yes, I suppose you're right.'

I wrote back to the owners of the club and said that, although I appreciated the invitation, I must gracefully decline.

In the end, the club never opened. It was never really a viable option in such a small place as Barrow-in-Furness. The men who were likely to visit those clubs would want to do so anonymously, but, in a small town like ours, news was bound to travel back to their wives and girlfriends if their fellas were seen there, and then there'd be hell to pay. PC Ollie said that most of his colleagues down the nick were disappointed. I think he was joking, but I was never quite sure with Ollie.

However, I didn't share the objections of a colleague in another town who spoke out against a branch of the sex shop chain Anne Summers opening down the road from his church. I'd visited the branch in Lancaster with Lesley on a number of occasions. I'm no prude, and I think the church as a whole tends to come over as far too repressive in matters of sex.

*

Fiona came home for part of the summer, which was lovely even if she did moan constantly about having to work to supplement her student grant. For someone who was always complaining about not having enough money to live on, she didn't do so badly. I was horrified to discover that, while she was complaining about not having enough to eat, she'd spent £75 on hair extensions. I told her that she should try eating them, but she wasn't impressed. She loved being a student, immersing herself in the culture of clubbing and parties. She was proud of the fact that I was a priest, loved telling people that she was a vicar's daughter and would always leap to my defence if anyone started mocking vicars. But, inevitably, what I dreaded most had happened. Fiona had a boyfriend.

She wanted to bring Paul home to meet us. My heart sank. I do not know why I was so surprised and despondent. She'd just turned nineteen and, despite the fact that she was still my little girl, she was also a young woman.

I lay on the bed, having one of my 'I'm not ready for this,' moments. Lesley just kept smiling at me, shaking her head and telling me not to be so silly.

'Mark, she's only bringing her boyfriend home for a couple of nights, just so that we can meet him.'

'I know, I know. I'll be charming when he arrives. I just feel that I'd like more time to get used to the idea,' I laid my right hand on my forehead.

'Now who's being the drama queen?' Lesley lay down beside me. 'Come on, Mark, you're blowing this out of all proportion.'

'Well, he's got to sleep in Johnnie's old room. There'll be no hanky panky while I'm around.'

'Of course. Fiona isn't like that, you know she isn't. Anyway, she probably expects you to patrol the landing all night. She knows what you're like.'

'Oh, I will, don't you worry! One creak of the floor boards and Ringo will be sent packing.'

'Stop it, Mark! His name's Paul, not Ringo, and I'm sure he's a very nice lad.'

'He's from Liverpool, isn't he?' I wasn't going to give in. 'So I'll call him Ringo.'

Lesley was still lying beside me. 'I know what'll cheer you up,' she said.

I turned on my side to face her. Our noses were almost touching.

'What?'

'How about a dress rehearsal?' she asked.

Now I was definitely interested. 'Ooh! What are you going to wear?'

'Not me,' said Lesley, pushing me away, 'You've got sex on the brain. I meant the twins. We need to give them a dress rehearsal for their new school uniforms. It won't be long till September.'

It was the last straw. I threw myself back on the bed and put both hands over my face.

'Oh, Lesley, my babies are starting school and my daughter's bringing her boyfriend home! Everything's changing! I'm past being cheered up,' I wailed.

*

Despite my reservations, Paul was a nice lad. He looked half asleep most of the time and I don't know if he'd ever heard of combs - his hair could've done with having one run through it from time to time. He didn't take offence when I called him Ringo, either.

He reminded me of myself a little, when I first started courting Lesley. I hoped that that was where the similarities ended, though, because at his age I was an unemployed former psychiatric patient with no prospects. I didn't mind him being Fiona's boyfriend, as long as it was not serious. I took him to one side during his stay and simply explained, in the nicest possible way, that my daughter was very precious to me and I hoped that he would treat her right otherwise I might be a little upset. I think he understood what I meant!

Fiona told me later that he'd been petrified of meeting me, particularly because I was a vicar. I had thought about playing up to the stereotype, putting on horn-rimmed glasses and false teeth and inviting Paul to join me for evensong. I think he was pleasantly surprised to discover that, apart from being an over-protective father, I was quite normal. The twins loved him and were all over him and he was very good with them. I felt quite sorry for him because Fiona was forever keeping him waiting while she did her hair, nails and make-up and tried on endless clothes. He was quite prepared to go to town looking as though he'd just crawled out of bed.

In lots of ways, as the relationship developed, Paul was very good for Fiona and gave her the emotional support she needed. However, within fifteen months cracks started to appear in the relationship, and Paul eventually dumped her. Fiona was inconsolable for weeks, drinking herself into oblivion before eventually returning to the nest for some TLC. My heart ached for her and I wanted to go and sort things out between her and Ringo, but she and Lesley both told me to stay out of it. Eventually Fiona settled down and went on to complete her studies, obtaining a degree in tourism and leisure. I was so proud of my princess.

By the end of September the twins had settled down very well to the new routine at St Pius Catholic School. They looked so cute walking to school in their new red uniforms, even if it was a bit of an ordeal getting them into them. When Lesley worked nights I did the school run and it was a real kerfuffle getting the twins to co-operate in the mornings. Once I was so frazzled that I accidentally dressed Mark Jr in the wrong top, pulling it distractedly over his head while he watched cartoons. The top was red, the right colour, but it was his old nursery jumper, not his new school pullover. Not long after I'd got home after having dropped them off, I had a call from his teacher explaining that Mark was inconsolable, having just discovered that he was wearing a baby jumper. Would I bring his St Pius' jumper to school for him to change into?

At first Lesley and I missed the twins dreadfully, but, like them, we soon got used to the new routine and really appreciated having a few hours of peace and quiet. But we always looked forward to picking them up, despite the noise, chaos and laughter they brought home with them.

*

Lesley and I had decided to become partners with KCM, contributing money on a monthly basis out of the tithe which we always set aside for supporting God's work. There was no doubt in our minds that Ken Copeland's ministry was having a profound effect upon our lives. Despite the challenges, the trials, the heartaches and the uncertainties, the year since I'd first come across his teaching had been the best year of my Christian life and ministry so far. I felt alive and in touch with God in a way that I had not believed possible. Life was good and Lesley and I felt extremely blessed. We'd discovered that prosperity was not just about money but was much more to do with spiritual wholeness, wholeness in body, mind and spirit. As time went by, my insecurities, fears and sense of inferiority diminished. My time in the spiritual wilderness changed into a new area of abundance and overflow in the spirit.

Lesley herself began to embrace Ken Copeland's teaching with great effect. Her constant preoccupation with balancing the books and her ever-present worries about money ceased as she began to discover that God really was our source and supply and would meet our every need. The principles we were discovering were spiritual laws, which always worked when we did our part – obeying God. For the first time in my spiritual journey I was learning all about the blessings which are ours in Christ. We moved from scepticism to being converts to what is sometimes known as the Faith Movement. I knew that Ken Copeland had his critics, but, as far as I was concerned, his teaching was responsible for pulling me out the pit of despair and giving me back my life, my marriage and my ministry.

Changes were afoot during the latter part of 2006, as St Matthew's was finally going to get its own priest, three years after David, the former rector, had left. The Rev William Dean, curate of St Mary's, Walney Island and the son of a retired arch-deacon, was to become what was known as Priest in the Parish. He couldn't be Vicar, as I was already the team vicar and was senior to him. He and his family moved across the water and settled into the vicarage next to St Matthew's church.

Following the appointment of William Dean to St Matthew's, the Rev Stuart Evason, Vicar of St James, the next-door parish to St Francis and St Matthew's, would be made Rector over the newly-formed team of three churches and would oversee William and myself. The archdeacon was very keen for the new team to come into effect as soon as possible.

I'd be lying if I did not admit that I felt a little uneasy about the planned changes. I'd never really been a team player, much preferring to do things in my own way and my own style. That was how things had worked between me and David, the former rector, and it had suited us both very well. We got on with our own jobs but we were always there to encourage and support each other when the need arose. However, I was prepared to give the new order a try and looked forward to welcoming William and working with Stuart within a team. It would be nice, I thought, to have colleagues to meet with for mutual support and the sharing of ideas.

*

William Dean's induction and licensing service was full of the usual pomp and ceremony. The local clergy were an impressive sight in their robes as they joined with various dignitaries and members of the community to welcome William and his family to the parish. The church bells rang out and there was a lovely, spontaneous round of applause as the archdeacon led William to his stall. But, despite a good service and a terrific tea afterwards, I was in a sombre mood when I returned home. Things were going to be very different now.

The former rector, David, and his wife had successfully introduced young families into the church, expanding the Sunday school and children's activities so much that by the time they left the parish there was a waiting list. The services David led were always joyful and lively, if rather chaotic and disjointed. I knew that his approach had annoyed some of the traditionalists, who wanted to turn the clock back to the kind of services where children were seen but not heard, where the singing was dirge-like and there were endless dreary readings and liturgical responses. I had admired and respected David, an evangelical and charismatic man who was full of the Holy Spirit. He had bridged the gap between the church and the people in the community very well. After he left, during the years of interregnum, I had tried my best to maintain his ethos, but there was a lot of opposition and sadly many of the families David had introduced to the church left. The children's work had dried up as a result.

And now, here was William. I knew that he preferred the High Church tradition of dignified, formal public worship, although I also knew that he was keen to meet Stuart and myself for prayer and had talked about pulpit sharing between the churches.

I could not quite put my finger on why William's induction service had left me with an uneasy feeling. Lesley and I sat in the kitchen with our cups of coffee and I tried to explain it to her.

'The usual crowd was there, swooning all over the bishop. The archdeacon was being obnoxious and giddy, making silly remarks about William knocking me into shape.'

'You're kidding!' Lesley looked surprised.

'Yes, can you believe it? William's only been ordained five minutes.' I pulled a face. 'But that wasn't the only thing. The bishop thanked everyone by name for their help over the last three years in keeping St Matthew's going during the interregnum. Everyone except me. He didn't mention me once.'

'Well, that is odd. What did the archdemon say?' Lesley joked.

'Ha, ha. Freudian slip! The arch*demon* went on about celebrity culture and said that that has no place in the church. I thought for a moment he might be having a pop at me because of my high profile in the Evening Mail.'

'Now you're being paranoid,' said Lesley firmly.

'I suppose.' I sipped my coffee moodily and remembered that William hadn't seemed impressed when I'd shared my spiritual awakening with him. He'd looked uncomfortable when I laid hands on his head and prayed for him and his ministry. And when I mentioned my former depression and suicide attempts, all he'd said was that he couldn't relate to them because he'd never been depressed.

'Mark, I'm sure everything will be fine. You're just feeling a little insecure because of all the changes that are taking place. Why don't you put one of your Ken Copeland CDs on and spend some time in prayer?' suggested Lesley, standing up and rinsing out the coffee cups.

'I'd rather come to bed with you, sweetheart,' I said, trying to look appealing.

'That's not the answer, Mark, and you know it. You need to get before God and deal with any problems straight away. Do not let the devil in.'

She was right. You cannot stop the birds flying around your head, but you can prevent them from building a nest in your hair. The old 'birds' of insecurity, fear and inferiority were circling round me and I had to take authority over them and stand on my faith, in Jesus name. I was just getting started when I was interrupted by the phone ringing.

'It's Peter,' Lesley said, handing me the receiver.

'Peter? What on earth does the rural dean want at this time of night?'

'Not Peter the rural dean, you twit, it's Peter Braithwaite from Duddon Inshore Rescue. I'm going to bed. You make sure you pray when you've finished talking to him,' Lesley said commandingly, and left me to it.

Peter was just starting to explain that he was picking up some radio transmissions from Liverpool Coastguard when I heard his pager go off in the background, followed immediately by my own in my pocket.

'Immediate launch, person reported,' read the message.

'Peter, I'll pick you up in five minutes!' I slammed the phone down, shouted 'I've got to go!' up the stairs to Lesley, and rushed out. Prayer would have to wait. I climbed into my blue Vauxhall Vector Estate, activated the emergency lights and sped off into the night, pleased to be able to put the day's concerns behind me and help save lives.

*

I had celebrated Mass in the Lady Chapel at St Matthew's on Wednesday mornings for the last three years. Although the congregation was small, I always enjoyed the informality and the banter between us. So I was pleased that William had agreed to let me take one last service before he took over the reins completely. He said he would simply sit with the rest of the congregation and take the sacrament from me. I thought this would be the start of the development of our team ministry, of sharing services and swapping pulpits.

After the service, William and I walked over to his vicarage together. I couldn't help but notice that he was rather subdued.

'Is everything OK, William?' I asked as he put the key in the door.

He did not answer, and I had the feeling that he was trying to work out what to say to me. He left me in his study while he went to make the coffee. I'd never seen the room look so tidy - when

David Kennedy lived there you could not even see the carpet and there were always piles of books and papers on his desk. Now, academic-looking tomes about the Blessed Virgin Mary, various saints and the priestly calling were ranged neatly on the shelves and everything looked as though it had a place and was in it.

William returned with a tray of filtered coffee. He set it down on a low table and settled himself in the armchair opposite me. He still hadn't said a word, so I asked him again if everything was all right.

'Who taught you to celebrate Mass?' he said.

What a strange question, I thought. 'My training vicar, Ian Davis, of course. We had quite a few runs through together before I did it by myself. Why do you ask?'

'Just curious,' he said, getting up to pour the coffee and handing me a mug.

I thought no more of it and went on to make polite conversation, asking him how he and his family were settling into the parish and telling him how much I was looking forward to working with him. We agreed that the two of us and Stuart from St James would meet for evening prayer in the Lady Chapel at St Matthews every afternoon around 4pm for half an hour whenever we could. We'd take it in turns to lead. I was looking forward to having fellowship with my new colleagues, but I felt uneasy after I left the vicarage. I found William's long pauses rather intimidating.

For the next few weeks we did indeed meet for evening prayer. It took me a little while to get used to the structure, as I had not used it for some time, and I felt that this frustrated William, who was very methodical and liked things to be done properly. He was very patient, even helping me to find the pages. As the weeks passed and we started to get to know each other, I began to enjoy myself. I felt we were beginning to gel as a team.

But it was not long before I discovered, to my surprise, that William was still asking one of the retired priests to take services for him when he was away. I decided to ask William about this one afternoon during evening prayer.

I caught up with him just before he entered the church and launched straight into what was on my mind.

'William, I thought we'd agreed that when you were away I would take your services for you? Especially the Wednesday one, which you know I've been doing for the last three years.'

He looked at me and hesitated.

'Yes, we did have that conversation,' he agreed, opening the church door.

'Then why are you asking someone else to do it?' I asked.

'Does that bother you? Do you feel excluded?'

'I don't want to appear paranoid, but yes, I'm beginning to feel that way,' I said.

Before we could continue the conversation Stuart arrived, so we all went into the Lady Chapel and took our seats for evening prayer. After we'd finished we sat in silence for a moment, in thoughtful reflection.

William broke the silence. He turned his back on me and spoke to the rector.

'Stuart,' he said, 'Mark was asking me, before you arrived, whether I've been excluding him from taking services at St Matthews. As you know, I was very angry at the way he celebrated Mass a few weeks ago when I sat in the service. In my opinion, Mark allows his personality to distract from the solemnity and sanctity of public worship. As priests, I believe we should leave our personalities at the door of the church. So yes, I am excluding him.'

I could not believe what I was hearing. I just sat with my head lowered. When he'd finished speaking, I picked up my baseball cap and keys, brushed past him and Stuart and left without saying a word. It was only later that I felt angry and regretted not saying anything in my own defence.

Under the teaching of KCM I'd learnt to avoid strife and conflict with other people. So I felt that it was best to offer the situation up to God and keep walking with him in love. The old me would have risen up like the Incredible Hulk and, quite frankly, done something unbecoming to a clerk in holy orders. Lesley was proud of my response, even though she felt that I should go and talk to the archdeacon.

For the next few weeks and months I continued to go to evening prayer and dutifully attended all the staff meetings with William and Stuart, the rector. I tried to maintain cordial relationships with them both. None of us mentioned what William had said. To be honest, I didn't want to discuss it, and I felt that a dignified silence was the best way to proceed. It was important to me to continue to put into practice the new, scriptural teaching I was learning, about faith expressing itself through love. Having struggled with anger for years, the last thing I wanted to do was re-ignite that emotion.

So I kept coming before God in prayer to say sorry, whenever I felt like reacting angrily or defensively. It was not easy, and I admit that there were times when I wanted to have my pound of flesh. But I resisted the urge, trying to put into practice the teaching of Jesus and serving St Francis church and the people of Ormsgill with the same dedication, commitment and passion as I always had.

There was no doubt, though, that relations within the newly-formed church team were already strained.

*

In the middle of all this, I was due to officiate at my nephew Simon's wedding down near Scunthorpe. It had been in the planning for over a year and I was looking forward to it, partly because it meant that Lesley and the twins and I could get away for a few days.

When the big day arrived, I felt so proud of my family. The twins looked cute in their little waistcoats and Lesley was a knock-out in a clingy new dress. My dear nephew looked so nervous as he stood in front of me, waiting for Paula to join him at the altar, while the joyful notes of '*Here Comes the Bride*' rang out from the organ. I felt very conscious of my golden cope and couldn't help remembering that the last time I'd been in church with Simon had been on my own wedding day, twenty-three years earlier. Simon had looked angelic, dressed in a sailor-suit, but he had fidgeted and asked questions throughout the entire service, finally shouting at the top of his voice that he needed the toilet!

It was good to get the family together again, although I'd been a bit nervous at the prospect. I had not seen my sisters Jenny and Maxine and their husbands since my Dad's funeral. When we got to the reception, Maxine gave me the biggest hug ever, which was lovely – although she nearly squeezed the life out of me! Jenny was more restrained, but we had a good chat and she was great with the twins. My brother Paul was still suffering from depressive anxiety disorder, but he'd come over for the day from Wales with a friend from his church.

The twins had a great time and held centre stage on the dance floor until they almost brought the three-tiered wedding cake crashing down! Fortunately my sister Shene was on hand to steer them away, then stand guard in case they came back... Mark Jr had been stopped in the nick of time from taking a premature bite of cake – when I looked closely I could just see the indent of his teeth in the icing.

*

Back in Barrow, I turned all my attention to working within the new team. An added pressure was the knowledge that my contract was coming up for renewal. I very much wanted to stay within the diocese. I'd come to love Barrow-in-Furness and felt at home there. Just the thought of having to leave brought all my childhood insecurities rushing back to the surface. But now I knew that I had to deal with them and not allow them to affect me. I knew I had to keep feeding my faith every day if I was to face the future with confidence in God.

CHAPTER TWELVE

The archdeacon was due to visit just before Christmas. The church needed to prepare an inventory of all the silver and all the church ornaments in advance of his arrival, and the registers and church buildings all had to be made ready for inspection. Fortunately, it was the responsibility of the church wardens to make sure that everything was in order. Usually I tried to keep out of the way, but this year the archdeacon's visit had special significance for me. I knew that he would be outlining the procedure for the review of my ministry and listening to what I had to say about wanting to stay in Barrow so that he could submit a report with recommendations about me to the bishop.

I kept looking out of the study window to see if he had arrived. Lesley walked in as I was on my knees on the floor, fiddling with my swivel chair.

'What on earth are you doing, Mark? You're not trying to sabotage that chair, are you?'

'Ha, ha. I'm just lowering it.'

Lesley gave me one of those puzzled looks I'd grown accustomed to over the years.

'Why?'

'Basic psychology. If the archdeacon sits in a slightly lower chair than me, I won't feel so intimidated by him,' I explained. I was trying to lock the lever into place so that the archdeacon would not be able to raise the seat.

'Hmm. Mark, you never fail to amaze me,' said Lesley. She sounded disapproving. 'Anyway, here he is!'

I shot up off the floor, cracking my head on the desk on my way up.

'Aargh, that hurt!'

'Serves you right! God's judgment!' said Lesley with glee.

I peeped through the blinds of the study window and sure enough there was the archdeacon, walking up the path with his official-looking briefcase in his hand.

'Shall I go and put the kettle on?' enquired Lesley, her hand on the study door.

'No! Don't do that Les - I don't want him getting too comfortable! The sooner I can get rid of him, the quicker we can go for lunch with Shene and Graham.' My sister and brother-in-law were in the middle of a visit to us and we'd arranged to go out to lunch together that day.

I checked myself in the hall mirror: dog collar in, shirt tucked in, shoes polished. Taking a deep breath, I opened the door.

'Hello archdeacon. How nice to see you! Do come in.'

'Hello Mark, are we in the study?' he asked cheerfully, brushing past me.

I followed him meekly, then stopped in my tracks. He'd headed straight for the wrong chair!

'Um, wouldn't you be more comfortable in the other chair?' I enquired, without much hope, before sinking, defeated, into the chair I'd so carefully lowered earlier. The arch-deacon already looked pretty comfortable where he was, towering above me in my bigger, wider, and altogether grander, black leather Star Trek Captain's Chair.

I sighed inwardly and attempted to pull myself together. I certainly didn't want to lose the opportunity to make my case, so I launched straight into my speech, making sure that the archdeacon understood how settled we were as a family, how much we loved Barrow and the surrounding area, and how St Francis' church had been growing under my ministry. As I talked, I felt myself getting quite emotional. The roots I'd made in Barrow were so important, not just to me, but also to Lesley and the children.

As I talked I kept half an eye on the archdeacon's pen, flowing across the pages of his notebook. I did feel intimidated by him, but that was probably just as much to do with the problems I'd had since my childhood with relating to authority figures, as the fact that he was sitting in my chair.

He looked up when I stopped talking.

'Thank you, Mark. I can see how passionate you are about your parish. There's no doubt that your ministry has made a huge impact on a very deprived area. You've given me some good reasons for wanting to stay in Barrow, which I will of course take into consideration when I write my report for the bishop.' He put the cap on his pen, closed his notebook and leant back in the big chair.

'Do you have any questions?' he asked.

'Yes! Now that you've heard my case for remaining in Barrow, will your report be in favour of my license here being renewed?'

'Sorry Mark, that's one thing I can't tell you at this juncture. Due process has to be followed, so I need to hear the views of the church council and meet with the church wardens and the other clergy of St Francis and St Matthew's.'

My heart sank. I wasn't convinced that everyone would want me to stay, simply because I felt that there had been some resistance to my ministry since I'd rediscovered my faith. I decided to produce my ace card.

'Archdeacon, are you aware that the bishop wrote to me last year, saying how happy he was for me to remain in Barrow? He said he felt my gifts and ministry are well suited to the town.'

'I know, Mark. But I still have to follow the correct procedure.'

Ironically enough, I could see the bishop's letter from where I was sitting. I'd laminated it and stuck it to the wall in my study, where it was just visible over the archdeacon's right shoulder. The sight of it did nothing to calm my nerves - my stomach was churning as I silently tried to pray and draw on my faith.

I could feel the archdeacon looking at me. He asked quietly, 'Mark, how are you getting on with William?'

'Fine,' I answered. 'We meet with the rector for evening prayer every day and for a staff meeting once a month. William's style is different from mine, but I'm not knocking that. He's obviously very gifted and talented and some people clearly prefer his more formal and traditional approach to worship. I'm more spontaneous, but that's the beauty of the Church of England, isn't it, arch-deacon? Clergy come in all shapes and sizes.' Stop it, Mark, I told myself, as I started to ramble on.

'Are you sure there haven't been any problems between you?' the archdeacon persisted.

'There has been a bit of a personality clash. But it's like any new relationship, it takes time to get to know each other. To build mutual respect and...'

The look in the archdeacon's eyes brought me to a sudden stop.

'I'll be honest with you, Mark,' he said. 'The renewal of your license will depend on how you are functioning within the team ministry.'

I wished someone would beam me up. This interview was not going how I'd hoped. Instead, I explained the whole situation as clearly and as honestly as I could, while my visitor listened sympathetically.

When I'd finished, the archdeacon said he'd like to take me and William out to lunch together.

'I'm sorry, archdeacon, but I've already arranged to have lunch with Lesley and my sister and brother-in-law today,' I told him. He was clearly disappointed, and, like an idiot, I decided to defend my corner.

'Had I know that you wanted to take me and the boy-wonder out today, archdeacon, I would have made different plans,' I heard myself say. I apologised immediately but I knew the damage had been done. From now on, however much I said I respected and wanted to support William, the archdeacon was bound to remember that one ill-judged, defensive comment. The 'boy wonder' would stalk my future.

*

I sighed with relief as I showed him out of the house.

Lesley appeared in the corridor as the door closed.

'How did it go?'

'I think my fate has been sealed,' I said gloomily. 'I'm sure there's a plan afoot to remove me from Barrow.'

'Are you sure you're not being paranoid again? I love you, Mark.'

'I love you too, Les. But…'

She stopped me by putting one finger on my lips. 'Shush. Come on, Mark. You have changed so much in the last fifteen months. You've become a real man of faith. I love seeing you in action as a priest. You treat people with such warmth and love that they cannot help responding to you and trusting you. Listen to me, Mark – I want you to know that our future depends on God, not on the archdeacon or the bishop. It may be a bit rough ahead, and I expect there'll be all kinds of uncertainties, but don't lose sight of what you've been learning. Stand on your faith, believe in God's word, deal with your fears and kick the devil where it hurts. OK?'

She hugged me tight. I felt a sudden rush of love for my faithful and loving wife and was just starting to return her embrace when the door bell rang, making me nearly jump out of my skin. We were standing so close to the front door that I could peep out through the spy hole without letting go of Lesley.

'I don't believe it! He's done it again. Look who it isn't!'

Lesley stretched round me, looked and giggled.

'I'll go and put the kettle on and find the biscuits. You'd better let him in,' she said, heading for the kitchen.

'Hi Ollie! Come on in,' I said, opening the door to reveal Ormsgill's favourite policeman. Ollie listened carefully as I told him about the archdeacon's visit, what had been happening in the church since William's arrival, and my fears for my future in Barrow.

'What will you do if you do have to leave?' he asked when I'd finished.

'I'll cross that bridge when I come to it. My future is in God's hands and I know he won't fail me.'

Ollie gave me a look. 'Hm, that American guy seems to have done you some good. I don't understand it, but if it works for you, go for it!'

'It'll work for you too, if you give it a chance, constable,' I said.

'Don't you start preaching at me, Father Mark! They still call me God's cop down at the nick because of you!' Ollie laughed, getting up to go.

'Where are you off to now?' I enquired.

'To the bunker. But first I'm going to the pie shop.'

'I wish you wouldn't call your office the bunker! You're not under siege, you know.'

'Sometimes it feels like it. Someone even pinched the blue light from above the door the other day. Anyway, before I go, there's some good news you might be interested in.'

'Don't tell me – they've made you Chief Constable of Ormsgill!'

'I already am! No, I'm finally getting some help. All the campaigning you've done on my behalf has finally paid off. I'm getting a new Community Support Officer. He's only twenty-three and still wet behind the ears, and what's more he's a Geordie. But I'll soon knock him into shape. I'll be bringing him round here when he arrives.'

Once Ollie had gone I realised how hungry I was.

*

After evening prayer that same afternoon, William came over to me.

'Mark, I had lunch with the archdeacon today. You and I have both had our knuckles rapped, and I want to apologise for hurting you.'

I have not had my knuckles rapped, I thought, but if William is gracious enough to apologise to me, I can certainly be gracious enough to accept his apology. I held out my hand and smiled.

'No hard feelings, William,' I said, as he took my hand and shook it.

'I apologise for hurting you, Mark, but I do not apologise for what I said,' William continued, in an even tone. I felt my smile fade as our hands dropped to our sides.

Later that evening, I picked up an email from William. He made some suggestions as to how we could move forward. He apologised again for hurting me, but stood by his opinion that my personality detracted from the sanctity of the priesthood and should be left at the door of the church.

I thought that email was a good way for us to correspond. It gave some time for reflection and would hopefully prevent either of us from saying things in the heat of the moment that we might later regret. After consulting with Gerald, my longstanding friend and spiritual director, I emailed William saying that I was happy to respond positively to all his suggested ways of working together. I concluded: 'However, there is a fundamental issue to be resolved about which it seems we cannot agree.

'It is a fundamental catholic teaching that the validity of the sacraments is unimpaired by "worthiness" of the celebrant. I do not know a single priest in the Church of England who is capable of leaving his personality outside the church door before celebrating. It is a human being, not a robot, who arrives at the altar. Even a priest who attempts to celebrate Mass in a depersonalised way is, in fact, expressing his personality through the very process of depersonalization.

'I do think that either you will have to accept me as the "impaired" human being that I am, or seek some image of perfection elsewhere. I hope, though, that we can now draw a line under what has happened and look forward to the future, working together in a spirit of reconciliation and love, for the sake of the kingdom of God and for the sake of the newly-formed St Matthew's, St Francis' and St James' team ministry.'

And that, as far as I was concerned, was the end of the matter; neither William nor I raised the issue again.

*

The meeting with the archdeacon, the church council and my colleagues from the team had been arranged for Sunday 18th February at the rector's house. The previous day had been a lovely one for the time of year, sunny and warm, and I felt very peaceful.

Seated around the oval table in the rector's dining room were my two church wardens from St Francis and the two church wardens from St Matthew's. The rector and the arch-deacon were there already. I made polite conversation and submitted to some ribbing from the church wardens, but my stomach was starting to do cartwheels.

When William arrived, the archdeacon welcomed everyone and then said something which alarmed me.

'We don't expect Mark to move out of the vicarage immediately!' He laughed briefly at his own joke, but I felt sick and wondered what could be coming next. I did not have to wait long to find out; he invited me to join him privately in the rector's front room so that he could go through the report with me before returning to the oval table to discuss it with the rest of the team.

'Here you are, Mark.' He handed me a copy and we sat down opposite each other.

The word CONFIDENTIAL was typed across the top in bold red capitals. I read the first paragraph, which outlined the procedure and the code of practice. I noted that members of the church council had been invited to write to the archdeacon to express their views. The report went on to say that twelve letters of support had been received from key people in the community, including the Barrow MP John Hutton, the Mayor, the leader of Barrow Council, the Inspector of Police and the Duddon Inshore Rescue station officer David Caldwell. I was surprised to discover that, apart from my two church wardens, no one from the St Francis' committee had been invited to express their views.

It was clear from the evidence, I read, that my ministry had made a real and positive difference to the life of the parish and the community, which had been greatly valued. All very positive, I thought. But the next line said that the purpose of the consultation was not to review the effectiveness of my ministry. Now, to be honest, that did surprise me.

I glanced up. The archdeacon sat motionless in his chair, watching me impassively. The following paragraph outlined the future of the team ministry, and got very technical concerning future strategy. I skipped quickly to the next section, which expressed the view that the future of the team as a whole couldn't be ignored in making any recommendations about the renewal of my license.

'Therefore it is regrettable that the relationship between the two clergy most active in the team remains strained,' I read. My heart sank. The church wardens felt that my gifts and character were not best suited to team working and my style had not contributed to building up trust across the team. By now I knew what was coming. All the church wardens and the other team clergy unanimously believed I should only be offered a limited term of renewal of license.

The archdeacon's recommendation was that my license - my clergy contract - should only be renewed for two years. However, he also strongly recommended that I should begin to consider my future immediately, with a view to finding a new parish.

I felt as though I'd been kicked in the stomach. What hurt most was the feeling that I'd been betrayed by my own team.

I did not go back with the archdeacon to the oval table, but returned home to tell Lesley the news. She and I both knew that I'd have to draw on all the resources of my faith to emerge from this time of trial strong in the Lord.

*

That evening I lay on the bed in silence, unable to contribute to family life. All my old insecurities were surfacing, with a vengeance. I simply couldn't imagine life outside Barrow, or St Francis. Deep down, I was still afraid of the unknown.

Once Lesley had got the twins to bed she came in and sat down beside me.

'How are you doing?' Her voice was gentle.

'Sick to my stomach.'

'Mark, I feel like that too. But I also feel a sense of peace.'

'I wish I could be like that, Les, but I feel so hurt. It's just like the time when I was told I had to leave the children's home.' Waves of despair and rejection were beginning to wash over me. I could feel their approach and was powerless to resist.

Lesley folded me in her arms.

'Oh Mark, don't. You've done nothing wrong.'

I wanted to drown in her love and comfort.

'We'll get through this together, with God's help,' she said, and I felt her body straighten up.

She let go of me.

'Come on, don't stay lying here, feeling depressed. Put a CD on, open your Bible and start to fight back.'

'I will.' I tried to summon a smile. 'I just need some time to think and deal with my emotions.'

*

The next few days were difficult. I was danger of spiralling out of control. Fear and panic dominated my thinking, making me tearful and self-pitying. Lesley was worried for me, fearing that I might end up seriously depressed again. She began to lose patience and said I should go and talk to the rural dean, Ian Hook.

So, armed with a copy of the review, I went round to his vicarage. I liked Ian; we'd been ordained at the same time and had grown together in ministry. He took the report and began to read, pacing up and down his study.

'You're stuffed!' was his first comment. 'Yep... You're not even being offered another parish in this diocese. Yep, mate, you're well and truly stuffed!'

I wished he'd shut up, but in the end I couldn't help but smile. He was so right.

A few days later the assistant bishop came to see me and Lesley at home. Although he was sympathetic, and understanding of how frightening it must feel for me to be told that I had to leave St Francis and Barrow within two years, he said that it was unlikely that the bishop would overrule the archdeacon's recommendation. He said I should focus on the next two years as a positive affirmation of my ministry, and I had plenty of time to complete my current work and find a suitable appointment elsewhere.

I decided that enough was enough. I'd done all the mourning I was going to do. Emotionally, I was spent – and Lesley was about to crack my head open if I did not get up off the canvas and back into the ring. She kept coming into the bedroom, sitting on the end of the bed and quoting scripture to me. It reminded me of the time in the children's home when I went on hunger strike. The house parent I had had a crush on came into my bedroom armed with a tray of food and demanded that I eat. Lesley was doing the same, only this time it was spiritual food she was ordering me to eat. She was right. It was time to fight back.

Later that evening, when everyone was in bed, I sat at my desk and repented of giving in to fear and anger. I began praying in the spirit and worshipping God. I was interrupted by Joshua, who said he was having nightmares and couldn't sleep. I held him and told him not to worry, Daddy would take care of him. Everything would be all right. I lifted him gently up into my arms and carried him back upstairs.

'I love you, son,' I said, and gave him a kiss as I lowered him down onto his bed.

'I love you too, Daddy.' He threw his arms around me.

I tucked up him securely then went over to Mark Jr's bed. He was sound asleep. I kissed him lightly on his warm cheek. 'I love you too, Mark Jr,' I whispered.

Back in my study, I turned on the CD player and listened to a teaching tape. As I listened, I heard God speak into my spirit. He said, 'Mark, just as you held your son in your arms and told him you love him, I hold you in my arms. I love you. Take hold of my word and trust me for your future; I will not fail you.' Tears of joy flowed down my face as I sat at my desk thanking God for reminding me that whatever bad things had happened to me, he could and would turn them around.

CHAPTER THIRTEEN

The bishop had stressed the importance of continuing to apply myself to my ministry in Barrow, while trusting in God's provision for my future. I could not argue with that. So I tried my best to carry on as usual, ministering to the people in the church and community, and working together with the rest of the team in the parish.

One of the good things that had happened recently was the arrival of a Police community support officer, Matthew McFall, to assist PC Ollie on the Ormsgill estate. Matthew was about the same age as my son Jonathan, and just as tall and thin. A typical youngster, he'd arrived on the estate with a bang, announcing that he was going to clean up Ormsgill. Not surprisingly, this had not gone down too well with the residents – or PC Ollie! Never one to hide his feelings, Ollie made it clear to everyone, including his superiors, when he was irritated or fed up. He gave Matt all the mundane jobs, like giving out and collecting the crime survey forms, but Matt was so laid back that he occasionally forgot to do them. Ollie, not one to shirk his duty though, did his fair share and more than made up for Matt's forgetfulness. The twins loved Matt, because he'd often pop in and help them sort out their X-Box when they couldn't get a game to load. Lesley treated him like a son and could never resist trying to feed him up.

Matt gradually won everyone over, including the somewhat over-sensitive PC Ollie, and the Ormsgill community. He became a much respected PCSO and eventually went on to become a full constable.

Ollie and his colleagues were astonished that I was leaving.

'You're being blackmailed with God,' Ollie said. 'It's a stitch-up, if you ask me. Everyone knows how good you've been on the estate. Crime is down – what more do they want? It's the kind of political manoeuvre I'd expect from the powers that be in the police force, but not in the church. Unbelievable. That's what it is.'

My relationships within the community were as strong as ever. As the news that I would be leaving began to spread, various community groups started to get up petitions for me to stay in the parish. Although I was flattered by their loyalty, I steered them away from taking direct action. I knew it would not help, and would not make any difference to the decision that had already been made about my future.

Relationships within the church were more difficult. I still valued and respected the church wardens: they did a good job, and I continued to affirm and encourage them, maintaining a professional working relationship although I knew they had supported the archdeacon's recommendation that I should leave.

I had informed the whole church during the Sunday morning service of the result of the archdeacon's review. Some people were visibly stunned and upset. Members of the St Francis' committee were angry because they had not been consulted, while the St Matthew's church council had been. Members of St Matthew's congregation who supported my Thursday services were just as shocked and saddened as most of my own congregation.

Trying to be positive, I reminded people that I had two years left, so I would make the most of them. What I did not tell them was I had already begun to look for another post and was scrolling through the church's situations vacant advertisements weekly.

On the morning of the twins' fifth birthday, March 19th, Lesley sat at the kitchen table scanning the Church Times' jobs section.

'Hey! Look at this, Mark.' She handed me the paper, tapping one of the adverts with her finger.

I read, 'Priest in charge of the parish of Bardsea, Lindal and Pennington, and deanery youth officer.'

I sat down and thought for a minute.

'Hm, it's three churches – and a part time youth worker position.'

'Mark, you could do it easily. Two of the churches are very small, and you've had plenty of experience of youth work,' said Lesley. I could see that she was trying to encourage me.

'Think about it,' she continued. 'You could stay with Duddon Rescue – it would be no further than Barrow for you to respond to a call-out. I could stay in my job: in fact it'd be only just round the corner. The twins could probably stay at St Pius', and Mark Jr would still be near the hospital. Come on, you've got to apply!'

She had a point.

'OK, sweetheart. I'll get the application form after the boys' party. If I'm in a fit state to do anything by then, that is!'

After the party, when the twins were finally tucked in bed and sleeping the sleep of the exhausted, I emailed the archdeacon requesting an application form for the job. I was quite excited at the prospect of working in a semi-rural parish with a strong sense of community and still being close to Barrow-in-Furness. But although I filled in the form and sent it off promptly, I heard nothing. The closing date for applications came and went. Still nothing.

Eventually, an email arrived from the archdeacon headed 'application/interviews'. I opened it with excitement. At last things were moving forward.

'Dear Mark,' I read. 'You were the only applicant for the post of priest-in-charge, therefore, having failed to attract another candidate, it is with regret that I write to inform you that we are no longer advertising this vacancy. Your application will be kept on file and, should we re-advertise in the future, it will be given due consideration. In the meantime I would encourage you to look further afield for a new position and seek a meeting with the clergy appointments advisor.'

To say I was disappointed would be an understatement. I could not understand why, just because I was the only applicant, I wasn't being offered an interview. But, strangely, despite my disappointment I still had a tremendous sense of peace in my spirit. I knew that God was in control, so I rested in that knowledge. All I could do was commit the whole thing to God in prayer and carry on with my life. What would worrying achieve? As Jesus said, worrying cannot add a single second to our lives, so why do it? Worry had no part in my new life. Whenever it surfaced I would deal with it – ruthlessly, if necessary.

*

Our twenty-third wedding anniversary was a particularly memorable one. We'd both been looking forward to a meal out with Trevor, one of the crew from Duddon Rescue, and his wife Gillian at a country restaurant Lesley had chosen. One of the biggest changes in my relationships since my spiritual renewal had been in the way I got on with Trevor. We'd never really seen eye to eye, and I hadn't really tried to make friends with him, preferring to keep him at arm's length. Gradually, though, the barriers between us had broken down and we'd become the best of friends. Everyone noticed that my attitude towards Trevor had changed dramatically.

On the evening of our anniversary I'd been struggling with a cold for a few days and was fast losing my voice. Lesley was definitely looking forward to having a meal without me talking endlessly throughout it. She picked out my wardrobe for the evening – jeans and a nice T-shirt. No dog collar for once. I'd only just shaved my head, so I looked a bit of a thug.

We arrived at the restaurant in good time. It was a lovely spring evening. Through the window we watched some horses in the field opposite. Some people were attempting to round them up and load them into horse-boxes, but the animals were having none of it and kept cantering off. We were so engrossed in watching them that we didn't notice it was almost two hours since we'd arrived, and over an hour since we'd finished our starters. My voice had now almost completely disappeared and I was reduced to whispering, which I found frustrating, although everyone else thought it was hilarious. In the end, Gillian politely asked the young waitress when we could expect our main courses, and was told that they'd be with us in no more than fifteen minutes. After twenty-five minutes I got up and went over to the waitress and told her it had been more than fifteen minutes. She looked very hassled and I felt sorry for her.

Finally our meals arrived and Trevor immediately began to tuck in. My plate contained mushy peas, not the garden peas I'd ordered. I whispered that I didn't want mushy peas and the waitress took the plate away. Minutes later my order returned, carried by a rather large gentleman. As he handed me my plate, he said, 'Would you mind not swearing at the waitress.'

'What?' I whispered, somewhat taken aback.

'Please don't swear at my waitress.'

I was indignant. I never swear.

'I'm a vicar. I don't swear,' I whispered at him, as he walked off.

And then without warning, both Lesley and Gillian erupted. Before I could stop them, they'd rushed off to the kitchen, full of righteous indignation, demanding an apology. From the other side of the restaurant, all I could hear was Gillian and Lesley shouting, defending my honour. In all my twenty-three years of marriage I'd never seen Lesley behave like this.

Trevor was quietly polishing off his food. Everyone else in the restaurant was looking over at our table, then over to the kitchen door. I had to do something.

I followed my two champions into the kitchen, where the waitress was in tears, insisting that I had sworn at her. Lesley and Gillian kept insisting that I hadn't. With no voice it was difficult to make myself heard, but eventually I was able to calm everyone down. It turned out that it was all a misunderstanding – when I'd whispered to the waitress, 'It's taking longer than fifteen minutes,' she thought I'd said, 'You're taking the piss.'

When we eventually got home and said goodbye to the babysitter, I sat downstairs and tried to work out what had just gone on. I was proud of Lesley for defending me but could not help thinking that if I'd been wearing my clerical collar instead of looking like a member of the British National Party, maybe things wouldn't have spiralled out of control in the way that they had.

Lesley had left me downstairs while she went and got ready for bed. She reappeared dressed in her long red dressing gown, and perched on the arm of the settee.

'Are you OK, darling?'

'Just a little shell-shocked! But thanks for defending me.'

'I love you more than ever, Mark. I love how you are growing in your faith. I love to hear you listening to your CDs and see you spending so much time with God. I love the way

163

you are with the twins. I just love you so much. There was no way I was going to let someone accuse you of something you hadn't done.'

'Looking like a skin-head probably didn't help,' I said, putting a hand on her thigh.

'I know what'll help take your mind off this evening,' Lesley said, standing up. Her dressing gown fell to the floor. 'Come on Mark, let's make this an anniversary to remember.' I followed her upstairs to the bedroom.

*

A few weeks later I had a visit from the archdeacon. He had a position he thought I might be interested in: team vicar in Askam-in-Furness. This surprised me a bit, given what I knew about the archdeacon's opinion of me as a team player, but I was elated at the thought of working in Askam. Askam was the home of Duddon Inshore Rescue, and I later discovered that the vicarage actually overlooked Duddon estuary. I was immediately convinced that this was God's answer. It sounded perfect.

I could hardly contain my excitement as I waited for the interview. I was so convinced that this was God's will that I stopped listening to him about it. Unlike Lesley. She was always more cautious and restrained than I was, and far more likely to weigh up the pros and cons carefully before taking action. She was also listening to God, as well as praying about the situation. But I felt that she was being far too negative and draining my confidence. We had a huge row.

On the first day of the two-day interview I was nervous but excited. I knew that one other candidate was in the frame, but I still felt that this parish had my name on it. The church wanted a young priest with a family, who would connect with the community and bring new people into the congregation. The profile of the person they wanted seemed to play to all my strengths. At the informal buffet to meet the members of the three parishes, the rector and the church wardens, I met the other candidate as well. He was a charming, self-effacing man – but he was over sixty.

The formal interview the following day was a rapid affair – I was in and out in under fifteen minutes. Alarm bells should have started ringing immediately – the other candidate was in the interview room nearly twice as long. I did feel slightly uneasy, though: I had a feeling that if I was appointed, they'd want me to give up the lifeboat.

Lesley and I sat out in the summer sunshine that evening, waiting for the call. I was still joking about measuring up for the curtains in our new vicarage, when the phone rang.

'I'm very sorry, Mark,' said the archdeacon. 'They've decided to appoint the other candidate.'

I felt the colour drain away from my face. Lesley came and stood beside me. The archdeacon said again that he was sorry, and suggested that I talk to the assistant bishop for a debrief before continuing my search for a new parish.

Over the next couple of days I went on a serious downward spiral. I was stunned. I really believed this had been God's answer, a perfect way of keeping me near Barrow and involved with Duddon. I felt under spiritual attack.

Lesley, Davo and my closest friends all rallied round. The Ken Copeland prayer department prayed for me and sent words of support and encouragement. I began listening to God again, and then the miracle happened. Within forty-eight hours, I was back on top, laughing and dancing around my study with Lesley, praising God. I'm sure part of the reason for this fast turn-around was the fact that I'd been feeding my spirit with the word of God, developing and building up my faith, laying good foundations so that when a storm hit, I had the resources to deal with it.

I still had some unanswered questions about the interview process, but I was beginning to think that God had prevented me from making a huge mistake. On reflection, I did not think the rector and I would have got on. We already knew each other, and the archdeacon had agreed that there might be personality clashes between us. But I'd been so convinced by the location that I'd suspended my critical faculties, shut God out, and steamed ahead regardless.

Finally I accepted that we were going to have to leave Barrow. Despite everything, I felt strong in my faith. I knew I needed to put into practice the principle of boldness in prayer, asking for the desires of my heart and obeying, trusting, worshipping and believing in God. I would pray. I would read the Bible. I would listen to God and worship him in spirit and truth. I would believe in order to receive.

No sooner had I decided this than we were plunged into another family crisis.

We were used to Mark Jr being in and out of hospital for short spells. It was always the same. He would be admitted, taken care of and then discharged. Usually he responded to treatment within a week and within two weeks was well enough to be discharged. This time it was different. He was rushed into hospital and the normal procedures were followed with military precision. Lesley moved into the hospital and I continued with my work in the parish while taking care of Joshua. Then, after about a week, Lesley called.

'Mark, please come straight away, I need you.'

'What's wrong, love?'

'Mark Jr isn't responding. They've moved him to the high dependency unit.'

Within ten minutes I was sitting beside Lesley, holding Mark Jr's limp hand.

'He's been like this since last night,' said Lesley. 'We thought he was getting on as normal and turning the corner, then suddenly he went floppy and his oxygen intake dropped. He cannot keep anything down.'

I looked at my little boy, lying there unresponsive and struggling to breathe. I held Lesley's hand and we prayed for Mark's healing. Between our tears, we thanked God that he could make our little boy whole.

Over the next few days there was no change. Lesley and I were exhausted. Joshua still needed taking care of, so we stayed at the hospital in shifts.

Everyone at the hospital was doing their best for him. Mark's nurse was marvellous: she had looked after him since he was a baby and had built up a wonderful rapport with him. This time, even she looked concerned, as his alarm kept going off when his oxygen intake dropped. None of the usual drugs that were being pumped into him were having any effect. A CAT scan was ruled out by his consultant because it was considered too expensive. We were told that they were considering ventilating him and transferring him to Alder Hey children's hospital in Liverpool, as he might need an operation to check the surgery he'd had at birth. They wanted to make sure that there was no tear in the membrane, which could be responsible for the build-up of dangerous bacteria.

It was shocking news and we were naturally fearful. But we came against the fear and continued to believe for Mark Jr's healing. I spent a lot of time sitting with him, reading healing scriptures over him. It was heartbreaking: he was completely unresponsive and did not even know that I was there.

Eventually, a senior paediatrician decided that Mark should have the scan, which showed that he'd developed a serious strain of pneumonia and needed treatment with different drugs. Within days of starting the new treatment, he had turned the corner and was sitting up in bed making a nuisance of himself, shooting at all the nurses with the toy tank we'd brought him. Three weeks later he was home, and life returned to normal.

Summer came and went, and with the changing seasons came another opportunity for me to apply for the position of priest-in-charge of Pennington Bardsea, and Lindal, with the deanery youth officer's post. The closing date for applications was the end of November, with interviews scheduled for just before Christmas. This time around I was far more measured about the application. I did not assume anything, but committed it to prayer and carried on with my day to day duties in the parish and with the lifeboat. The closing date came and went. I waited. When I'd still heard nothing, I contacted the archdeacon. He told me that once again I was the only candidate, so they'd decided to extend the closing date and interview in January.

One evening, the house was quiet and I was sitting in the kitchen with my Bible open, praying and reading, when I distinctly heard God's voice in my spirit, saying, 'Mark, I want you to withdraw your application.' I was so astonished that I stood up and said, 'You must be kidding!' I dismissed it as tiredness, coupled with an over-active imagination.

However, as days wore on, the conviction that I should withdraw grew stronger and stronger. I had no peace at all. So, after much deliberation and prayer, I emailed the archdeacon, telling him that I probably was not the right candidate, and withdrew my application. As soon as I'd done that, my peace returned.

I made one more attempt to stay in Barrow, registering an interest in the post of rector at St Luke's, a team ministry encompassing three churches. This time the bishop himself advised me not to apply. I respected his judgement and withdrew. I later learnt that the diocese had appointed a female colleague. She was the only applicant.

*

'Fides nostra victoria' - our faith is our victory - became our family motto as we looked forward to 2008. The clock was ticking on my search for a new job as my license would expire in March 2009. I was beginning to believe that my dream posting would be a police chaplaincy together with a small parish. I'd often acted as unofficial chaplain to PC Ollie and his colleagues in Barrow, and felt very comfortable with that work.

The clergy appointments' adviser had helped me draw up my C.V. which was now circulating the entire country. And in the meantime, parish life continued as busily as ever.

I still loved nothing better than spending time on the estate, loitering in and around the post office and involving myself with young and old alike. I popped into PC Ollie's police office for coffee and into the school where I was governor, to give support where I could to the head teacher and other staff. Ormsgill still fascinated me. As a working class lad myself, I felt at home in its culture, and loved its people. And I felt very strongly that that was where the clergy ought to be – out on the streets and in among the people, getting involved with their daily lives, armed with nothing but the love of God.

It was early in January that my old friend Davo alerted me to a post in the diocese of Newcastle. A team vicar of two small village churches in the parish of Dinnington and Brunswick was required. He or she would also serve as part-time chaplain to Northumbria Police.

I could barely contain my excitement. I felt straightaway in my spirit that this was what I had been believing for in prayer for over a year, but my recent experiences had taught me to remain focused on God and not get carried away. Even so, when the application form arrived, together with the parish profile and job description, it was hard not to get as excited as a child with a new toy.

Within a week of filling in and sending off the application, I was called for interview. Lesley booked a little cottage for us to stay in during the two-day process. Two other candidates were being considered and I was nervous, but still trusting God. I felt at peace in my spirit and every time I felt fear, I stood against it in prayer.

On the first day of the interview, I arrived at Police HQ in good time to meet the senior police chaplain. Lesley dropped me off at the security gates then drove off with the twins to a nearby garden centre which had a play area. Standing in the main hall, surrounded by police memorabilia and pictures of the chief constable and his senior staff, I felt a bit overwhelmed. My hands were sweaty and my heart was beating loudly in my ears, but I hoped I'd be able to keep calm and not let nerves overtake me. I wondered what the other two candidates would be like, and whether they were feeling as nervous as I was.

I did not have to wait long for the senior force chaplain to arrive. A large gentleman wearing a dog collar and a police ID badge bustled through the double doors with a welcoming smile on his face. He grabbed my hand, shook it enthusiastically and told me that the other two candidates had dropped out.

'You were our preferred candidate on paper anyway, Mark,' he said. He suggested that Lesley and the twins should join us for a buffet lunch, which was laid out in a small conference room. The assistant chief constable and some ladies from the occupational health department came along too, and I was soon perspiring with the heat of the room, the stress of the occasion, and the added stress of having the twins running amuck and sabotaging my interview. Lesley was doing her best to keep them under control but all the time I was trying to listen to what people were saying to me, I could hear her ticking them off as they ran around like mad things.

No one was more relieved than I when lunch was over and the ladies and the assistant chief constable said they had to get back to work. The senior force chaplain followed them out, leaving Lesley and me alone with the boys. I was exasperated.

'Can't you keep those children under control?'

'I'm trying, but it's not easy on my own.'

'Well, I would help, but I'm a bit busy at the moment. I'm about to be interviewed for a job which I probably now won't get!'

'Where's your faith? I thought you said God had given you this job?'

'Boys, will you BEHAVE!' Just as the words left my mouth, the door opened and the senior force chaplain reappeared.

He clasped his hands together in a dramatic gesture, reminding me a bit of the late comedian Tommy Cooper.

'Well,' he said, 'you may not realise it, Mark, but that was your interview. And everyone here has given you the thumbs up.'

'What?' I exclaimed.

'They like you, Mark, and so do I. I would have preferred a woman, but you'll do!'

I looked at Lesley and she looked at me. We both laughed and gave each other a hug and a kiss.

'Will you put her down!' said the senior force chaplain, beaming at us delightedly.

He took us all on a tour of Police HQ and before we left he said that even if the church didn't want me, the police did and he would ask the bishop to find me a parish.

Thankfully Lesley took the twins off and kept them away while I met with the two clergy in the parish team. The meeting at the rector's house went very well, and after an hour's chat I had a look round the parish and the other churches before being dropped back at St Matthew's in the village of Dinnington to be shown round by the two church wardens. I do not know why I still felt nervous - they could not have been more lovely and charming. I felt such a warmth towards them that I knew that somehow God was in this. Everything seemed to be falling into place without me having to try and impress anyone. I was just being myself, not trying to hide my vulnerabilities, but trying to be as sincere as I could in expressing how I felt about everything I was being shown.

It was easy to be positive – I liked everything I saw. I was impressed by the people, who appeared just to want someone to love them and to help them grow as disciples of Jesus, as they reached out to the wider community. I believed in my heart that God was telling me that this was to be our new home.

Lesley and the twins arrived. As we were shown round the vicarage I was grateful that the boy next door played with the twins and kept them out of harm's way.

After a busy few hours, we had some time to go back to the cottage and rest and relax before meeting the members of the congregations of St Matthew's and St Cuthbert's for an informal meal at a local pub.

We took no chances with the twins for the evening meeting, taking colouring books, activity books, crayons, pens and pencils to occupy them while we chatted with everyone who'd come to meet us.

When we arrived, we were greeted like royalty. It was so lovely that I had a lump in my throat all evening. We felt completely at ease. Members of the congregation had even bought the twins a birthday present each, even though their birthday was still a few days away. I couldn't remember the last time I'd been treated with such kindness by a group of strangers.

Appointing a new vicar was a two-way street. They had to like me, but we had to like them. Throughout the evening people kept coming up to us and engaging us in conversation, showing a genuine interest in us as a family. Although Lesley wasn't the one being interviewed, she was charming and beautiful and talked to everyone. I'd never seen her blossom so much in a social setting. The twins sat all evening at the table doing their activities, helped by various church members. It was touching to watch. Before he left, the area dean told me that he was going to say a special Mass for us tomorrow, because he wanted us to come. He said he thought everyone else felt the same.

When we got back to the cottage, all I could think about was the passage from the Bible that tells us to delight ourselves in the Lord and he will give us the desires of our hearts. It was difficult to get to sleep, and for once I was not even interested in sex. After the twins were asleep, Lesley and I sat in the cottage kitchen around the pine table, chatting and praising God for answered prayers. We felt that the blessing of God was on our lives. It was a good position to be in before the formal interview with the bishop the next day. Excitement still kept me awake that night.

*

The one thing you should not be for an interview is late. But we could not find the bishop's house and had to keep stopping and asking passers-by where it was. By the time we arrived, Mark Jr was feeling sick.

The bishop's secretary opened the door to us and Mark Jr promptly threw up all over the hall carpet. I felt so nervous that I thought I might be sick too.

Someone went to get Mark Jr a bucket and we were shown into the lounge. The bishop arrived just as Mark was throwing up again. Joshua was in a particularly chatty mood. He took one look at the bishop and asked him whether he went to bed in his funny hat? Mark Jr looked up from the bucket and asked why he wore a funny hat in the first place, because it looked stupid! I was horrified. The bishop laughed and told me to follow him to the room where we were meeting the rest of the clergy team.

'Good luck, Mark,' he said kindly to me, as we set off down the corridor.

'We don't believe in luck, do we Daddy!' a penetrating young voice commented from behind us. Bless him, Joshua was right. We didn't believe in luck, but we did believe in the blessing of God. I looked back to see Lesley smiling at me.

The hour-long interview was intense and exhausting, but the people were as lovely and charming as they'd been the previous evening. At the end, the bishop asked me one final question.

'Mark, how would you sum yourself up?'

I remembered the words of John Pritchard, my former tutor and mentor, now bishop of Oxford.

'If I might quote the words of John Pritchard, "Mark's an unusual man",' I said. Everyone laughed.

Back at the cottage, all Lesley and I could do was wait. They were the longest three hours of my life.

At last, the phone rang. The bishop's words spoke straight into my heart.

'We want you, Mark,' he said.

I thanked him, put the phone down and burst into tears. Sobbing into Lesley's shoulder, all I could say was, 'They want me. They want me!'

CHAPTER FOURTEEN

Although we'd only been away from Barrow for a few days it felt like an age. The bishop's words, 'We want you,' were still ringing in my ears. It was the nicest thing anyone had said to me in a long time. It felt wonderful to be wanted, and I thanked God for his blessing. Lesley and I could scarcely contain our excitement. There would no official announcement straight away though; Church of England protocol meant that I was obliged to keep the news to myself until such time as it could be announced simultaneously in Newcastle and in Barrow.

Easter came and went, then I received notification from the Newcastle diocese that the announcement of my appointment would be made in all their churches on Sunday 13th April. I decided to make the announcement to the congregation of St Francis just before the final hymn at our service on the same day. It was hard: I was sad to be leaving Barrow and St Francis and all the people I'd grown to love.

But this wasn't the time to dwell on the past. My colleagues, William and Stewart, the rector, seemed genuinely delighted that I'd found a suitable position. I even had a congratulatory message from the archdeacon.

I've never been very good at handling change, and it was difficult for me to accept that my time in Barrow was fast coming to an end. The town was the first place I'd ever been able to put down solid roots. Our impending move was the biggest upheaval in my life since I'd left the children's home in 1978. And it didn't just affect me: Lesley also had to come to terms with letting go her life in Barrow, where she'd been working for ten years and made some very close friends.

Burning bridges and cutting ties is never easy, but it has to be done in order to move on. That's why I decided to stand down from my role as secretary and deputy assistant station officer at the Duddon Inshore Rescue. On the night of the AGM in May I handed back my uniform and pager, together with the secretary's box in which I'd put everything that the new secretary would need. I gave my report and said what a privilege and honour it had been to serve the life boat for six years. I knew how much I'd miss being part of such a fine crew. Station officer Dave Caldwell and former station officer Bernard McNamee both stood up and thanked me for the last six years, with Bernard saying that I had been the best secretary in Duddon's forty-year history. They presented me with a bunch of flowers for Lesley and a spy cam for my computer so that we could keep in touch. When I got home, I stripped all the lights and lettering off my car – the final act of closure on my lifeboat career.

'How are you feeling, Mark?' asked Lesley later that evening.

'Subdued.'

'I know – it's hard saying goodbye. Why don't you come up to bed? I'll help you take your mind off it…'

'Not right now, thanks, love. I'm just not in the mood.'

'I can get you in the mood. Promise.'

'I'm sorely tempted! But I think I'll just listen to some tapes and have a bit of time with God.'

'Well, if you change your mind, wake me up.' She gave me a broad wink, and went upstairs.

I tuned into a Believers' Voice of Victory broadcast on my computer. Just hearing the theme tune and watching the opening credits lifted my spirits, then Ken Copeland's voice rang out, 'I don't care who you are, I don't care how desperate you feel, God has the perfect plan for your life. He has a laughing place for you, a joyful place for you. Stay tuned for today's broadcast!'

Just what I need, I thought, settling back in my chair. Maybe after this I'll wake Lesley up, I chuckled to myself.

Before the final service at St Francis, there was a surprise leaving 'do' for me at Barrow police station. Lesley and I were summoned by PC Ollie and arrived to find not only him and young Matt, but also their colleagues, the inspector, the sub-postmaster and postmistress from the Ormsgill post office, and Jo Halpin from the Northwest Evening Mail. For once, I was speechless when the inspector handed me an American-style gold police chaplain's badge and a Commander's certificate of merit – a rare honour for a civilian. I was so touched by the kind things they said I could hardly take it in.

Then, finally, it was time for my last service and our last goodbyes. My church warden, a former army sergeant major, presented me with a financial gift from the church. He had a tear in his eye. I thanked him and asked if he would take my salute, which he did. He wished me well and said he would miss me. I knew I'd miss him too: although he'd supported the archdeacon's recommendation he had been a great church warden.

When the removal vans arrived, Lesley and I decided to take the twins over to Preston for the day to visit Davo. We certainly did not want two excited little boys 'helping'! It was late when we arrived back home and the removal men had left for the night. We were all tired and wanted to get to sleep, knowing that we'd have an early start the following morning. We'd arranged with the removal men that we'd let ourselves in via the French doors, but when I tried to put my key in the lock, it would not fit. The men had left the key in the lock and had posted the other set back through the letterbox in the front door. We were locked out.

I tried to kick open the door into the kitchen from the garage, but it did not budge. Then I tried to kick the front door in, calling the removal men all the names I could think of without actually swearing. After several attempts, the church warden arrived, with a spare key to the front door. I did not even know he had one!

We were all relieved and pleased to see him, until we discovered that my kicking had damaged the lock on the front door and now that key would not turn either.

In the end, I had to kick in one of the panels and crawl through, opening the front door from the inside. What a relief it was when it opened and we were all finally inside! Lesley put the twins to bed and I spent the rest of the evening repairing and repainting the front door.

The next day we had arranged to travel in convoy to our new home, stopping for lunch on the way. Both our cars were packed and the van was loaded. The vicarage was empty of everything except memories. I went into every room, closing my eyes for a moment each time, and remembering. I said a prayer before leaving and then it was time to go. Lesley had the cat and the guinea pig in her car, I had the twins.

It started to rain as I got into my car. Rolling down the window, I handed the keys to the church warden. Half way down the drive I stopped and looked back at the red brick building that had been my home, then at the church which I had served for so long. I knew I would take with me many fond memories of my time in the town.

Looking at the twins all buckled up in the back seat, I smiled and wondered how long it would be before they started asking, 'Are we nearly there yet, Daddy?' I drove out of the drive, past the church, through the Ormsgill estate, and didn't look back.

EPILOGUE

Just over a year after leaving Barrow-in-Furness, the Rev Mark Edwards received notification from the Cabinet Office that he had been awarded the MBE in the Queen's New Year's Honours list 2010, for services to the community and the voluntary sector in the Northwest. It was cited in the press that it was a long way from a Lincolnshire children's home to the steps of Buckingham Palace but that was the journey the Rev Mark Edwards undertook...

ABOUT THE AUTHOR

Mark Edwards was ordained in the Church of England in 1995. He trained at Durham University before being appointed to his first post as Curate in the market town Ulverston in Cumbria. He served his second curacy in Barrow-in-Furness before being appointed Vicar of his own Church, in Barrow. During his time in Cumbria, Mark served as Chaplain to the RNLI and crew member of an independent Lifeboat station. Mark is married to Lesley and they have four children and two grandchildren. In 2008, Mark was appointed Chaplain to Northumbria Police and Vicar of two village Churches in Newcastle upon Tyne. Alongside his parish duties Mark is a governor at his local school and although he was made redundant from his post as Police Chaplain in 2014, he still volunteers with the Police as well as working as a volunteer Medic with the Northeast Ambulance service as a Community First Responder. Mark was awarded an MBE in 2010 for services to the voluntary sector.